the Getaway

TABLE OF CONTENTS

Written by:
Zach Meston

Layout & Design:
Tim Davis

Additional Layout
Mike Vallas

Special Thanks:
Susan Nourai
Grant Luke
Ramon Concepcion
Scott Nyce
Brendan McNamara
Chun Wah Kong
Andrew Hamilton
Ravinder Singh
Ben Brudenell

Versus Staff
Matthew Taylor
Howard Grossman
Kay Smith
Anastasiya Polunina

ISBN: 0-7615-4257-4
Library of Congress Catalog Card Number: 2003100411

© 2003 The Getaway Sony Computer
Entertainment Europe. The trademark is used
with the permission of Alpha Omega Publications.

The Prima Games logo is a
registered trademark of Random
House, Inc., registered in the
United States and other countries.
Primagames.com is a registered
trademark of Random House, Inc.,
registered in the United States.

01 | CHARACTERS AND GENERAL STRATEGIES PART I

The Fugitive
Mark Hammond

Playable Character

A former member of the Soho-based Collins Gang, Mark Hammond is now on the run for the suspected murder of his wife Susie. Desperate not to be captured so he can free his kidnapped child, Mark is trying recklessly to maintain his sanity and freedom.

The Criminal Mastermind
Charlie Jolson

An aging East End gangster and head of the notorious Bethnal Green Mob, Charlie has a taste for the 'finer things in life" like classic Bentleys, Savile Row suits and fat Cuban cigars. But history has passed Charlie by and his London is one he no longer recognizes and in the underworld no one stays on top forever.

The Gang Leader
Nick Collins

Slick Nick epitomizes the modern business ethic of 'work hard, play harder'. The Collins Gang controls Soho's bars and are the only modern crew that has come near to the former notoriety of Charlie's Bethnal Green Mob.

The Triad Leader
Shan-Chu

Shan Chu (Bobby) Lee is a recent immigrant from Hong Kong and heads up the London based section of the 14K Triad. The Triads are responsible for protection rackets enforced on the Chinese community, immigrant smuggling and drugs importing.

The Vigilante
Frank Carter

Playable Character

A determined member of the elite Flying Squad, Frank Carter's ambition is to nail Charlie Jolson. Some of his superiors, however, do not share his obsession, so Frank must bend the law to bring the Bethnal Green Mob to justice.

The Assassin
Yasmin

A stunning brunette and former escort girl, Yasmin gets a kick out of killing men. She has never known a man who wasn't interested in her and uses her allure to lead her contracts to destruction. Beneath this icy pretense, however, lies the heart of a lost little girl.

The Yardie Leader
Jamahl

Jamahl is the head of the Yardie gang responsible for most of London's drug problems. Heavily involved with arms dealing, these guys are vicious and determined to abide by none of the 'Old Code' that Charlie Jolson pays lip service to.

The Psycho Nephew
Jake

Jake Jolson enjoys murder, prostitutes, and murder, but not necessarily in that order. Recently tagged for a pandering charge, Jake needs Uncle Charlie's help...again.

(2)

(6)

(8)

A Driving

Cars in *The Getaway* suffer front-end damage and rear-end damage. Front-end damage breaks down the motor, slows down the car, and eventually renders the car immobile; rear-end damage makes it increasingly difficult to see the turn signals that guide you to your destination. There are four stages of car "health":

(1) If there's no smoke coming out of the engine, your car is in perfect (or near-perfect) condition.

(2) If white smoke is coming out of the engine, it's mildly damaged, but it's only going to get worse; the more you drive, the more damage is done to the engine.

(3) If black smoke is coming out of the engine, it's heavily damaged, and soon to burst into flames. Boost another car with haste.

(4) If the car is on fire, very quickly press the CIRCLE button to get out of the car before you're set ablaze.

(5) You probably already noticed this, but cars in London drive on the LEFT side of the road, not the right. Put your North American driving habits out of your mind and remember to follow the flipped flow of traffic, especially when you're pulling into an intersection.

(6) Reckless driving--swerving in and out of lanes, smashing into other cars or pedestrians, and so on--will draw the attention of the rozzers, while safe driving won't. Put the hammer down and learn to deal with the consequences.

(7) You can get out of a car from either side. Press LEFT + CIRCLE to get out of the passenger-side door, and RIGHT + CIRCLE to get out of the driver-side door.

(8) Get used to driving the wrong way down a one-way road, and get used to driving in the middle of a two-way road, squeezing between traffic as it moves in both directions. You'll frequently call upon both of these tactics as you proceed through the missions. And don't be afraid to drive on the sidewalk--you're already killing people by the dozens, so a few more pedestrians won't have much effect on your karmic balance.

(9) When you're parking the car near a heavy-traffic area, get out of the door nearest the sidewalk. Stepping out into a busy road is asking to be a hit-and-run victim.

(10) If you boost a police car, press L3 to turn the siren on and off. The siren won't work if the car is heavily damaged.

(11) For the DC Carter missions, the only hazard you have to hurry about is gangster drive-bys. You can boost cars, hit pedestrians, and drive insanely without getting in trouble with the police, since you ARE the police.

(10)

(3)

(7)

(11)

GENERAL STRATEGIES

B — Gangsters

1 In addition to the cops, you're frequently targeted by gangsters. Gangster cars are always quick and agile, so outrunning them is rarely an option. Gangsters also pull up alongside your car and unload their guns into the vehicle, which rarely kills you, but which can thrash the car pretty good.

2 If you attempt to boost a car with gangsters in it--you can recognize gangster cars not only because of their models, but because they have both a driver and a passenger, while civilian cars only have a driver--the angry criminals get out of the car and assault you.

C — Healing

Your character's health is reflected by his appearance:

1 If the character is standing up straight and walking normally, he's in perfect (or nearly perfect) health.

2 If the character is hunched over, clutching his chest, walking with a slight limp, AND has small bloodstains on his shirt and/or pants, he's slightly wounded.

3 If the character is hunched over and weaving, clutching his chest, staggering instead of walking, and covered with blood, he's severely wounded.

4 To heal your wounds, walk up to any wall, either directly facing it or with your side to it. After a moment, your character leans against the wall, breathing heavily. With each moment spent against a wall, the character regains a bit of health. When the character stops leaning against the wall and standing up straight, your health is fully restored, and the bloodstains fade away. You can heal at any time and at any location with a wall, so use this technique frequently.

D — Hostages

1 You can take a hostage at any time: simply walk up to any person--policeman, civilian, or gang member--and press X. (Make sure you're not pressing the Analog Stick, or you'll roll instead.) You grab the person and turn him around, using his body as a human shield.

2 Movement becomes more difficult when you're holding a hostage, as you can't turn left and right. You can, however, move forward and left/right or backward and left/right.

4 Police officers won't fire on you, regardless of the type of hostage

you're holding, but thugs will.

5 Make sure you're facing your attackers when holding a hostage. If you turn around and leave your back exposed, your attackers will gladly shoot at you.

6 While holding a hostage, press TRIANGLE to draw your gun. You can auto-aim and manually aim at an attacker while holding a hostage. Police won't return fire, allowing you to shoot them dead, but gang members will, even if you're holding one of their own.

7 Press SQUARE while holding a hostage to dispose of your human shield. If you have a gun drawn, you'll shoot the hostage (in the head if you're holding a pistol, or in the back if you're carrying a machine gun). If you don't have a gun drawn, you'll snap the hostage's neck. The neck-break is an important tactic in missions where stealth is required, since it doesn't alert others to your presence as a gunshot does; use it in most situations.

8 For DC Carter, pressing SQUARE with a gun drawn will make him knock out the hostage with the butt of the gun, and pressing SQUARE without a gun drawn will make him arrest and hog-tie the hostage. Again, the non-violent technique is the quieter one. Another consideration is that knocked-out enemies will eventually wake up and alert their friends (your enemies).

E — Partners

1 In several missions, you have a partner. If a police or gang car pulls up on the left side of your car, your partner shoots at it. When you stop the car and get out, your partner gets out with you, and shoots any nearby enemies.

2 Partners never run out of pistol ammo, which is good, but they can't heal themselves, which is bad. Partners also have a bad habit of getting so obsessed with the act of killing cops and gangsters that they forget whatever mission it is that you're on. If you've boosted a new ride, pull up to your partner so he/she can immediately get into the car, instead of having to walk to the vehicle.

3 Make sure you don't accidentally shoot your partner, or he/she will shoot you right back, and keep shooting until one of you is dead.

(1)

(2)

(3)

(4)

F Police

(1) If you commit a crime in view of a police officer--driving dangerously, boosting a car, drawing a weapon, taking a hostage, et al--the officer starts to pursue you. If the officer gets close enough to you, he arrests you, thus ending your mission. (The officer might also decide to pistol-whip or shoot you instead.) It's very easy to avoid the more egregious crimes, but it's difficult to drive safely, so you should get accustomed to police pursuit.

(2) If you're in a vehicle, the police use various tactics to stop you: ramming your car (from the front and behind), putting up roadblocks, and laying spike-strips across the road. There are several methods you can use to ditch the rozzers:

(3) **Stop & Kill**. When a police car comes to a voluntary or involuntary stop, it's stopped for good; the rozzers are, for whatever reason, unable to rejoin the chase. Stop your car, wait for the cops to get out of their cars, and immediately take off, leaving them eating your brake dust. The cops might shoot out your windows or tires, unfortunately. For a more permanent solution, kill the cops and drive off in a newly boosted vehicle. Often, when you use the S&K strategy, the rozzers lose your scent (and broadcast their cluelessness over the radio), allowing you to proceed through the mission without further harassment.

(4) **Brake & Slide**. If a cop car pulls up alongside you, slam on the brakes (press Down on the Right Analog Stick for the regular brake and R1 for the E-brake). The cop flies past you, allowing you to turn around or get out and shoot 'em as you prefer.

(5) **Dodge & Weave**. The tactic of choice in missions where you're racing the clock. Veer in and out of traffic, attempting to lure the police car into ramming another vehicle or a fence. This strategy works best on a wide one-way road, where you have plenty of room to maneuver.

(6) **Turn & Burn**. When a cop car approaches you from the front, it usually swerves in front of you, hoping to make you ram into it. Anticipate this by driving in one direction, then veering in the opposite direction as the cop car does its swerve. You can avoid a lot of collisions with this simple trick.

(5)

G Rolling

H Stealth

① Press X while running to execute a roll; Hammond rolls forward, stands up, and immediately starts running again. This maneuver is useful for escaping close-combat situations and getting under certain obstacles.

② You can also roll into stealth mode. Press X while running, then press X while rolling. If you roll into a wall, you press up against the wall at the end of the roll. If you roll into a low object, such as a crate, you crouch behind it.

① Move against a wall and press X to enter stealth mode. While in stealth mode, you can draw or stow your pistol(s) by pressing TRIANGLE. If you're holding another type of weapon, pressing TRIANGLE casts it to the ground.

② You can sidestep in stealth mode by pressing left and right on the Left Analog Stick. You can also lean around a corner or doorway by sidestepping up to it, then pressing and holding in the direction of the corner or doorway.

③ When you're leaning around a corner, you can auto-aim or manually aim and fire at enemies and targets (such as explosives). When you're behind a corner, you can fire blindly around it by pressing SQUARE--hardly accurate, but occasionally effective, especially if an enemy is running through a narrow corri-

dor, or about to run around a corner and pistol-whip you.

④ You can stealthily move from one side of a doorway to another. Lean out into the doorway, then press X to cross to the other side.

⑤ Walk up to a low object and press X to crouch behind it. You can sidestep behind low walls, and lean and shoot from behind low objects. Press the Left Analog Stick and X to roll out of a crouch.

⑥ Press R1 or R2 while crouching to stand up and take aim; release R1 or R2 to resume crouching. Press SQUARE to blindly shoot over the top of the crate.

GENERAL STRATEGIES

02 | THE MISSION WALKTHROUGH
PART II

LONDON

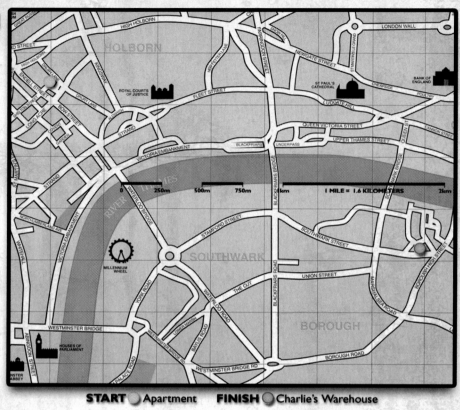

START ◯ Apartment   **FINISH** ◯ Charlie's Warehouse

Step on the gas of your green Alfa and pursue the red car of the "frightener." You'll never catch up to the bastards, no matter how skillfully you drive, but you can at least keep them in your sights.

① If you let the frighteners get too far away, you lose the mission. If you've smashed up (and slowed down) the Alfa, quickly steal another car and resume the chase. You'll hear a series of warning sounds, almost like a ticking clock, if you're about to lose the frighteners for good. (The best tactic, of course, is not to smash up the Alfa in the first place.)

② Slow down and watch out when you're turning around blind corners, and especially when you're driving the wrong way down a one-way street. It's all too easy in these dangerous situations to get into a head-on collision and obliterate your vehicle.

③ About a third of the way through the chase, the red car veers onto the right side of the road, then veers left around the corner. If you stay on the left side of the road, you'll smash into a "wall" of stopped cars. Either follow the red car onto the right side of the road, or drive on the sidewalk to the left of the traffic jam.

④ About two-thirds of the way through the chase, the red car drives down the center of a two-way, two-lane road. Squeeze through the traffic as you pursue it.

⑤ Near the end of the chase, the kidnappers really pour on the speed, smashing into plastic pylons as they drive down the center divider. You'll lose them at this point, but you're not far from the end of the chase; just follow the turn signals to find the red car parked in front of a warehouse. Get out of your car, draw your pistol, and walk into the alleyway entrance.

If you crack up the Alfa, waste no time boosting an alternative means of transportation and resuming the chase.

For the purposes of *The Getaway*, think of the sidewalk as a traffic lane.

Follow the trail of plowed plastic pylons to locate the frighteners' final destination.

A. Stand outside the door and pick off the two thugs waiting behind the truck. There's a third thug shooting at you from inside the warehouse, hiding behind a pile of crates, but he's too far away to hit you (or for you to hit him).

B. Press R2 to take manual aim, and shoot the red barrel at the top of the stairs twice. This blows up the barrel, and sends the thug hiding behind it flying through the air with his arse on fire. You can also shoot any of the barrels at the bottom of the stairs, which causes even more destruction (and also kills the thug).

C. Run forward and shoot the thug who comes out of the doorway, then take one of the guns on the ground to equip yourself with double pistols. Run to the bottom of the stairs and take the AK-47 that dropped to the ground when you blew up the thug at the top. (If you destroyed the stairs, the AK-47 is near the orange barrel; otherwise, it's in plain view.) Make sure you pick up the **AK-47** after taking the second gun.

D. If you need to relax after your first shootout, run over to the forklift and hop aboard. You can even shoot and blow up the forklift's

propane tank when you're done joyriding.

E. Run up to the right side of the door and press X to enter Stealth Mode. Now press LEFT to pop into the doorway and shoot the thug behind the crates. When you've taken him out, run into the warehouse and hide behind the pillar on the left. Lean around the corner and shoot the gray-shirted thug. Wait until a third thug charges at you from the back of the warehouse; lean around the corner and take him down, then take the shotgun he drops (but only if you prefer it to the AK-47, you nutter).

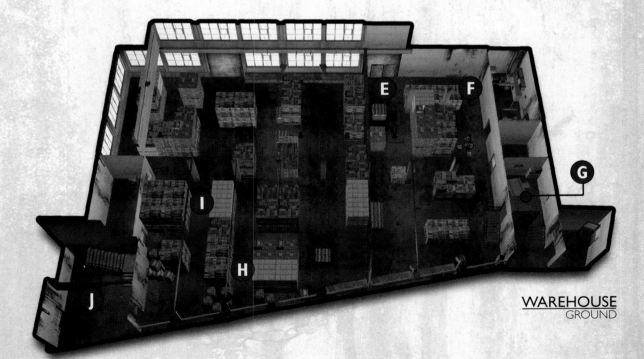

WAREHOUSE
GROUND

WAREHOUSE
FIRST FLOOR

F Now go to the left. Lean around the corner and shoot the thug on the small staircase, or blast the barrels under the stairs for a flashier disposal. A second thug comes out of the open doorway on the left as you walk toward the staircase, so be ready for him.

G Approach the stairs and shoot the thug who attacks from the right *if* he appears, which isn't always. In the room at the top of the stairs are two shotguns in a flattened crate. You should still have ammo in your AK-47 , but come back here and take one of the shotguns when you run out.

H Climb down the stairs and move against the wall to the right of the doorway across the room. Watch and wait for a thug to walk behind the pallets in the distance, then run into the room and hide behind either

pallet. Watch and wait for the thug to walk to the left, then run up behind him and press X to grab him. Make sure you're *not* moving when you press X, or you'll roll instead of taking the thug hostage. You can use the thug as a human shield, or simply press SQUARE to break his neck or blast him with your weapon.

I Slide down the row of pallets to the corner, then lean around and blast the thug, who really needs to pay more attention to his surroundings. Go left and around the corner, shooting a thug who comes out from behind the pallet.

J Run forward and through the doorway to find a dark staircase. Walk up the first flight, then turn left and blast the thug on the landing.

Continue to the top of the stairs, shooting a second thug in the doorway, and lean against the wall to the left of the doorway. Two thugs appear near the barrels; shoot the thugs *or* the barrels. Run forward and blast a third thug who runs around the corner.

K Run forward and lean against the wall just before the next corner. Two more thugs appear; stay behind the corner, and lean out to take your shots. When all three are dead, run forward and through the doorway, then turn left and enter the office.

G

I

K

LONDON

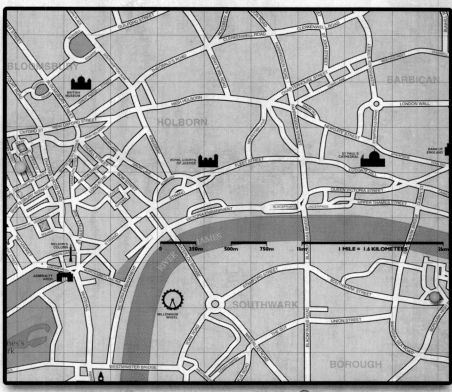

START ⬤ Charlie's Warehouse   FINISH ⬤ The Republic

You start the mission in a black Range Rover. You don't have to reach The Republic within a certain length of time, so the only choice you have to make is whether to drive by the rules of the road--through the 10 to 15 minutes of London traffic--or drive like a bloody wanker and get to the restaurant as fast as you can manage.

1 If you choose the Way of the Wanker, driving like a maniac and smashing through pedestrians, you'll inevitably draw the attention of the filth, who'll attempt to ram you off the road and stop you with roadblocks and spike strips. (You'll encounter at least one roadblock even if you're driving carefully, but you can go through it without drawing the fire of the police.) There's no way to shake the rozzers once they're onto you, unless you get out of your car and shoot every officer you see, then steal another car--but they'll probably continue to pursue you anyway.

2 Whether or not you have the police on your arse, keep driving toward Soho and The Republic, which is on one side of a long street. Look for a bald bouncer at the entrance.

Start

Care for a leisurely drive or would you prefer to pretend you're running the Paris-Dakar road rally?

If you tire of attempting to outrun the filth, pull over and eliminate them instead.

You won't need a cover fee to enter The Republic, but you will need to spill claret.

WALKTHROUGH

A Approach the bouncer, who tells you he can't let you in, and press X to take him hostage. (Don't do this when the police are driving past!) Draw your gun and enter the restaurant.

B Go around the corner to the left, where three thugs with pistols hold up their hands, hoping you won't kill their friend. (Sometimes, one of the thugs approaches you before you get 'round the corner.) Blast the foolish bastards before they get the drop on you, but keep in mind that once you start shooting, they'll shoot your hostage to get at you. You also need to take care not to let the thugs get behind you, where they can shoot you without hitting the hostage.

C When all three thugs are dead, take another hostage if you need or want to. By this time, your homicidal actions will attract the police, but they'll stay out on the street if you stay inside. (You can also go outside and shoot the filth, since no backup will arrive, and they won't shoot back when you have a hostage.) Walk back to the bottom of the stairs, turn

SOHO RESTAURANT
GROUND FLOOR

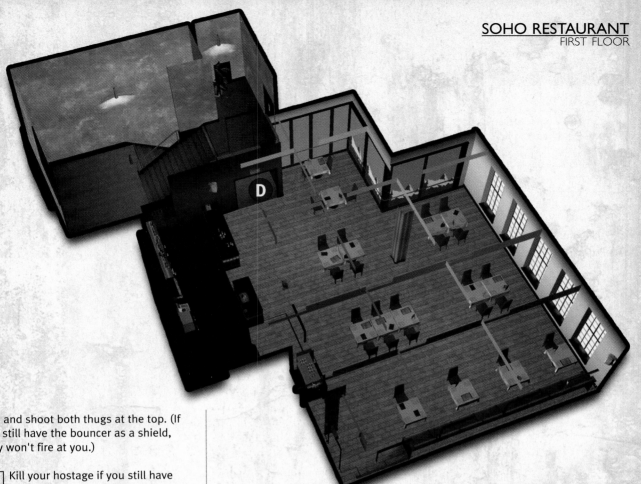

left, and shoot both thugs at the top. (If you still have the bouncer as a shield, they won't fire at you.)

D Kill your hostage if you still have one, because you can't traverse stairs when you're lugging around a human shield. Climb up until you're near the top of the staircase and press R2. Take aim at the bartender and shoot him in the noggin. (You have to blast through the windows separating you before you have a clear shot at him.) Make sure you don't get pushed out of position by fleeing innocents as they run down the stairs. Now turn left and shoot the bald thug behind the table; he might also come around the corner to attack you. Finally, shoot the blue-clad thug in the middle of the dining room. Walk behind the bar and take the shotgun the bartender planned to ventilate you with.

E Return to the staircase, continue climbing, and shoot the thug who comes around the corner. Climb all the way up the stairs and lean against the wall to the left of the doorway. Lean around and blast the seated thug, then shoot two more thugs as they charge at the doorway one after another.

F Move against the other side of the doorway, then lean around the corner and blast the thug behind the pillar if you can. Press R2 to aim and fire at the candle on the far wall, to the left of the mantle and the painting. When the candle explodes, you trigger a fire that slowly spreads until the restaurant is ablaze.

G Two thugs (or three, if you didn't kill the plonker behind the pillar) run toward the doorway as the fire starts to rage out of control. There's also a fourth thug inside the room, behind the bar on the right. When the fire alarm goes off, you've completed the mission.

Sitting down on the job is the last mistake that guard will ever make.

Stay away from the flames (which can set you alight) and the smoke (which can smother you) as you climb down the stairs. A thug attacks from around the corner as you reach the dining room, so be ready for him. There's also a cop at the bottom of the stairs.

Run outside and take a car--we suggest turning right as you exit The Republic and taking the Lexus--then drive fast and far away from the restaurant in any direction. Keep driving until the screen fades out, which means you've completed the mission.

Soho boys and police officers assault you as you leave The Republic.

WALKTHROUGH

SOHO RESTAURANT
SECOND FLOOR

LONDON

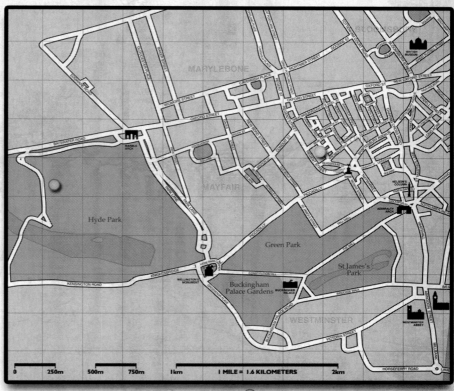

START ●   FINISH ○ Reptilian Gallery

Y ou start this mission with the vehicle you stole at the end of Mission 02. As you drive straight ahead from the starting point, a group of pissed-off Soho boys stops in front of you and proceeds to unload their AK-47s into your vehicle.

① If you're not in a hurry, return to The Republic, which is now totally engulfed, and steal one of the fire trucks. You can even run the siren. What fun! Now get back in a fast vehicle and head for Hyde Park, you nonce.

② Get to Hyde Park, fending off the Soho boys and the cops (if you're driving like a maniac and drawing police attention), and drive through the gate of the Reptilian Gallery. Park the car and enter the building *without* your weapons drawn, unless you want to provoke the Triads. (You can also try an excellent enemy-slaughtering technique as described below.)

Make the Soho boys pay for their aggression, then steal their weapons and their wheels.

Break the first rule of villainy and return to the scene of the crime for fire-truck fun and excitement.

Entering the Reptilian Gallery with a weapon is the most dramatic form of art criticism.

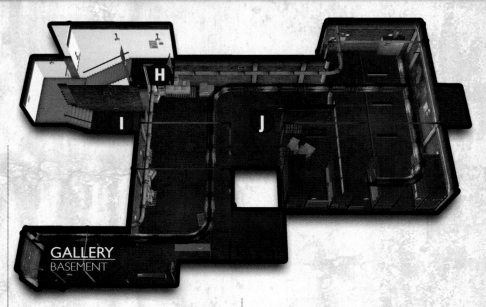

GALLERY
BASEMENT

A Walk up to the reception desk to have a brief chat with the woman behind the counter then, walk around the downstairs floor of the gallery and eavesdrop on all four pairs of visitors as they ramble amusingly about the exhibits.

B There are five Triads in the downstairs area, most of them wearing Chinese-logo jackets and baggy jeans, and you can kill them all without a weapon and without alerting anyone to your homicidal activities. The key is to wait until each Triad is out of the others' line of sight. You can even follow a Triad without arousing his suspicion. Just before making your move, press and hold R2 to look around and make sure no other Triads can see you or your victim. (It's okay if a visitor sees you--he or she runs out of the gallery, but doesn't scream or otherwise sound an alert.) Quickly press X to grab the Triad from behind, then press SQUARE to break the Triad's neck. Start with the Triad guarding the staircase (who can see almost the entire downstairs area), then the stationary Triad to the right of the entrance desk, then the three patrolling Triads.

C If you hear screaming and gunfire after snapping a Triad's neck, you've obviously been spotted, and it's time to let your pistols do the talking. Hell, if all the sneaking around isn't your style, just storm into the gallery with your weapon(s) in hand and start spilling claret. Or try this exceedingly clever technique: Stand outside the building and shoot the receptionist once, then let the five Triads attack you from the doorway. When you're done killing (for the moment), climb the stairs to the left of the entrance.

D Run toward the left-hand door and shoot the Triad who comes out of it, along with a second Triad behind him. (On rare occasion, neither of these gents appear; it's hard to predict exactly how many Triads will attack on the upper floor.) Move against the wall and wait, then press SQUARE to shoot around the corner as a third and (occasional) fourth Triad approach the door. Don't let them get on your side of the doorway, or they'll fracture your skull with several pistol-whips. Now move against the wall next to the right-hand door, then lean around the corner and pick off the Triad in the next room--who's usually, but not *always*, there. If you're feeling vandalous, shoot the glass case of the terra-cotta statue before you proceed (but don't stand too close to it, or you'll be wounded by the flying shards).

E Run forward to the room where you picked off the Triad. There's no sure-fire strategy in this area, which is a straight-up firefight between you and roughly half a dozen Triads, several of whom attack from the back of the room. Take your time, hide behind the walls, and shoot the Triads as they come at you (or as they cower behind the square white pedestals).

F Proceed into the next room and shoot the yellow-jacketed Triad on patrol, who could be in either corridor (but is usually on the right). Two more Triads might--but don't always--attack you

Plug a cork in the Reptilian Gallery receptionist and await the onslaught of upset Triads that follows.

This terra-cotta soldier is an ancient, priceless work of art, which makes shooting it that much more satisfying.

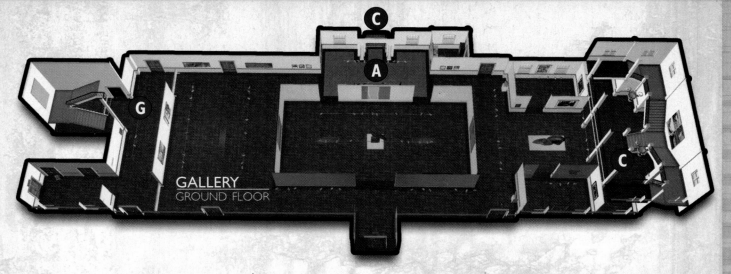

GALLERY
GROUND FLOOR

from the previous room, so be ready for them to appear.

G Climb down the stairs to the landing and shoot the two Triads. Climb down to the ground floor and go right, around the corner, to blast a third Triad (who's usually, but not always, there). Now turn around and walk through the open doorway.

H Kill the Triad on the stairs, then climb down to the landing and shoot the shotgun Triad around the corner. Before taking the shotgun, turn around and blast two Triads if they appear at the top of the stairs. (If they don't appear, keep moving!)

I Climb down the stairs into the basement. Move against the right side of the corridor, then lean around the corner to trigger two Triads into attacking you. (One's hiding behind the crate in the far-left corner, another behind the boxes in the far-right corner.)

Take the AK-47 the second Triad drops.

J Move against the wall and lean around the corner to trigger two more Triads to appear. Press [square] to ventilate the Triad on the right, then lean out to hit the Triad on the left. This triggers *four* more Triads to appear at the other end of the hall. Stay behind the wall and take them out with haste. Run around the corner after the carnage is complete to find the statue in a crate.

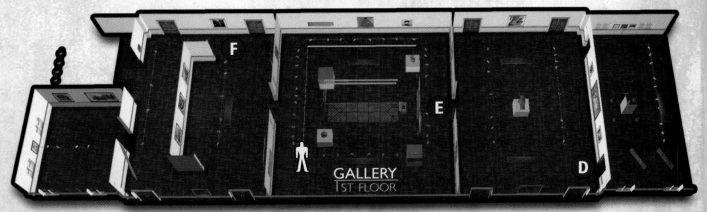

GALLERY
1ST FLOOR

WALKTHROUGH

LONDON

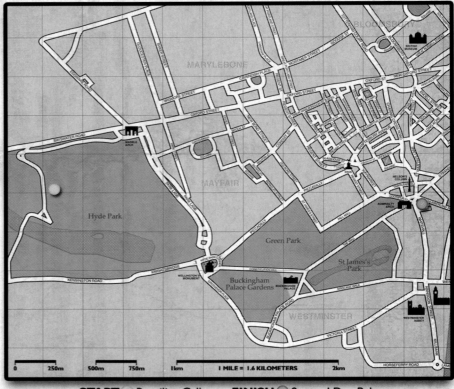

START ◯ Reptilian Gallery   **FINISH** ◯ Spotted Dog Pub

① You start the mission in the rear of the gallery, flying forward in a Renault Laguna, with two purple Honda Civics close behind you. Drive into the grass and stamp on the brakes, then get out of the car and blast the Triads. Take a healing rest against the entrance door, then steal whichever Civic has fewer bullet holes in it and drive toward the entrance. A third Civic attempts to block you, but you can easily cut around it to the right.

② On the first half of your drive to the Pub, you're chased mostly by cops. The police will surely wreck your Honda with their misplaced aggression, so be ready to bail the car, blast the rozzers, and steal new wheels. On the second half of the drive, you're chased and shot at by Soho boys in Lexuses. Keep going until you find the side street with the Pub. Approach it on foot or in a vehicle until the screen fades to black.

The Renault Laguna is an affordable vehicle--but you're not paying, so take one of the Honda Civics instead.

The rozzers will do everything in their power to prevent you from reaching The Spotted Dog.

LONDON

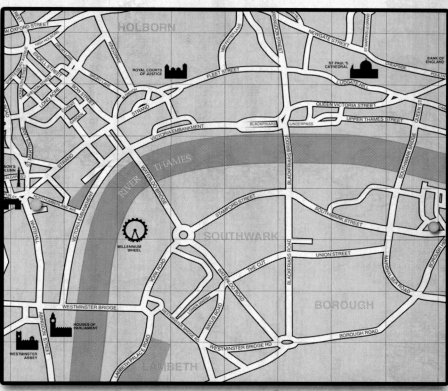

START ◯ Spotted Dog Pub   **FINISH** ◯ Charlie's Warehouse

G et into the car (a white Lexus) and Eyebrows appropriately hops into the shotgun seat. Eyebrows says to keep it "low-profile," but you only have three minutes of real-time to catch the van before the mission is aborted, so you *have* to drive like a wanker.

① You also lose the mission if Eyebrows is killed, which can happen if cops are shooting into the car, or if you foolishly decide to get *out* of the car (since Eyebrows gets out with you). Keep driving toward the van, doing your best to avoid collisions, and let Eyebrows shoot out the passenger side at any police car that pulls up alongside. (If you drive quickly and skillfully enough, you might never have a cop-car encounter.)

② You'll eventually make a left and spot the police van and its escort cars in the distance. Listen for Eyebrows's comment and watch your hazard lights to confirm that you've finished the first stage of the mission. Keep driving toward the van, and watch as a police car is rammed off the road and bursts into flame.

③ You now have three and a half minutes of real-time to ram into the police van until you've damaged it enough to complete the mission. You can smash into the van's rear bumper, but this doesn't hurt it at all. Instead, pull up alongside the van (watch for oncoming traffic, trees, etc.) and swerve into it *hard*. At worst, you'll cause some damage, as indicated by a trail of black smoke. At best, you'll make the van spin out and come to a stop, which instantly completes the mission. You'll hear a warning bell after three minutes have elapsed. At 3:30, the van kicks in the afterburners and flies through a police blockade, leaving you to try again.

If a rozzer pulls up alongside you, Eyebrows fires his pistol at the cop to discourage further pursuit.

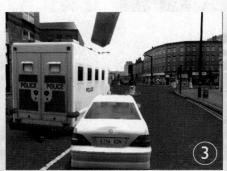

Hitting the police van from the rear is useless. Hitting it from the side is priceless.

Stop the van in under three and a half minutes, or be forced to attempt the mission again....and again....

WALKTHROUGH

WALKTHROUGH

LONDON

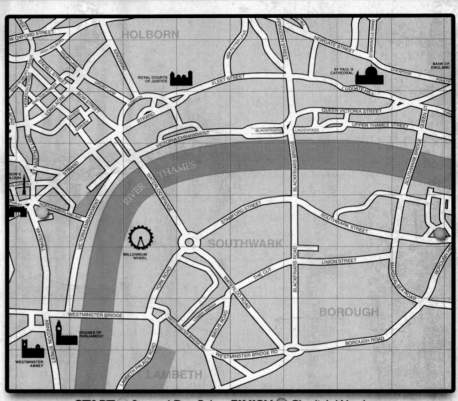

START ○ Spotted Dog Pub   FINISH ○ Charlie's Warehouse

① In this particular mission, the Lexus can take a good amount of punishment. You can get into a dozen head-ons without doing any damage to your engine--and even when your front-end is mangled beyond recognition and you're driving on wheels instead of tires, kicking up a shower of sparks. Literally all you have to do is keep driving until you reach the warehouse, then drive through the entrance.

The Lexus can withstand an impressive amount of punishment in this particular mission.

Drive the wrecked Lexus through the entrance of the parking lot to complete the mission.

Keep off the accelerator at the start of the mission and enjoy the demonstration of inferior shooting accuracy.

Start

A

B

A t the start of the mission, the old thug instructs you to stay put, but you're about to violently violate his instructions. Walk up to him while he's jabbering and press X to put him in a chokehold, then press SQUARE to snap his bloody neck. Mark Hammond doesn't take orders from tossers.

A This next thug is an optional kill, but it's fun, so: Turn and walk toward the staircase with the red barrels beneath it. Intercept the thug as he comes down the stairs, grab him, and kill him.

B Once you leave this section of the warehouse, if you're seen by a thug, the mission is instantly over. If you fire your weapon, you draw the attention of any nearby thugs, so keep your gun holstered. (You'll have many opportunities to spill claret later on.) Walk forward into the next section of the warehouse, and around the pallets. Approach the second thug from behind, grab him, and kill him with something other than kindness. (There may or may not be a weapon at his feet. If it's a crowbar, pick it up and use it!)

C There's a third thug within sight of the second thug you just killed; you can avoid him or kill him at your discretion.

Unnecessary violence? In the world view of Mark Hammond, there's really no such thing.

D If you want to snuff him, move up against the pallets, shuffle up behind him, and do the deed.

E Walk back to the body of the second thug, then turn left and walk to the window. You can see a thug inside the office, but he can't see you. This thug is an optional kill who yields a fun weapon, but it's a high-risk maneuver. Walk into the doorway of the office, and *immediately* move up against the window-wall before the thug catches you out of the

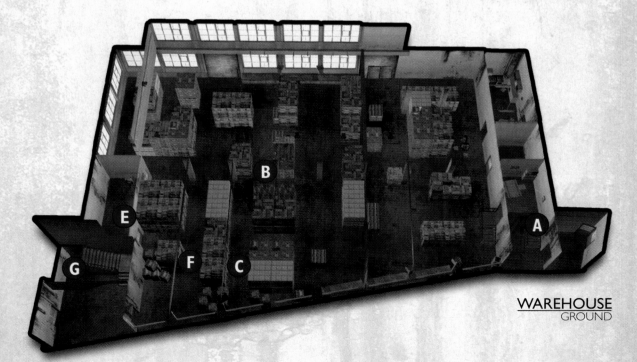

WAREHOUSE
GROUND

WALKTHROUGH

WAREHOUSE
FIRST FLOOR

D

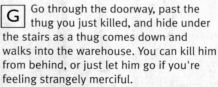

E

F

corner of his eye. Sneak behind the thug, kill him with a neck-breaker, and take his crowbar (or meat cleaver) from the floor. (If you don't kill the bald thug at the beginning of the mission, he appears in the doorway here.)

F Leave the office, walk up behind the next thug, and kill him with a neck-snap or a cleaver-whack. Easy enough!

G Go through the doorway, past the thug you just killed, and hide under the stairs as a thug comes down and walks into the warehouse. You can kill him from behind, or just let him go if you're feeling strangely merciful.

H Climb up the stairs to the first floor and move against the wall to the left of the doorway. Once the thugs walk away, move into the next room and crouch behind the low wall. Shuffle to the left and wait for a thug to take a peek in

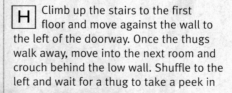

G

H

the window and walk away. When he's gone, get up, take your *own* peek in the window, and follow behind the thug.

I Approach the elder thug from behind and choke/chop him, then go through the doorway and kill a second thug. Return to the main corridor, move up against the wall, and sidestep to the corner. Listen in on the conversation, then run forward into Charlie's office.

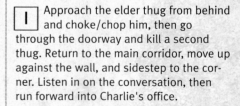

I

LONDON

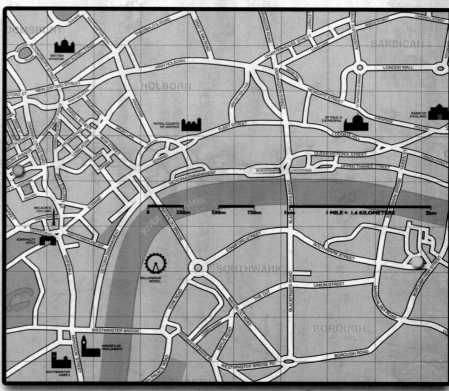

① There's no time limit in this mission; you just need to drive the green Honda Accord to the Siu Fung before the cops or Triads shoot you dead.

② When you reach the heart of Chinatown, drive toward the Siu Fung until the screen fades out.

START ○ Charlie's Warehouse   **FINISH** ○ Chinatown

Johnny Chai isn't a good conversationalist, but at least he's smart enough to wear a safety restraint.

The Triads won't be happy with your precious cargo, but such is life for an involuntary courier.

WALKTHROUGH

WALKTHROUGH

LONDON

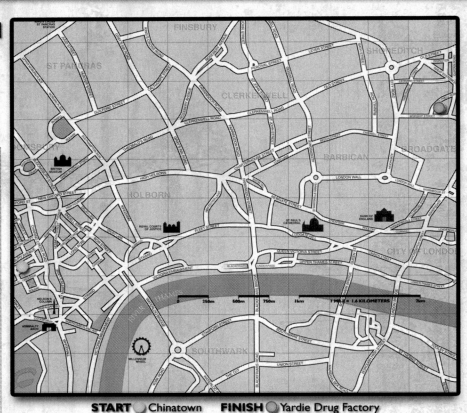

You were stuck with the green Accord in the previous mission, but now you can grab any car you like for the long drive to Holywell Street. We suggest taking one of the Triad's purple Hondas or black Nissans. You'll have to engage in a heavy-duty firefight to get one, however.

① No matter which direction you choose at the start, you'll have to run a gauntlet of Triads, whose shoot-em-up actions will draw the attention of the rozzers. During the drive to Holywell, you might have a Triad car on one side of you and a police car on the other. The Triads and cops will shoot at each other, so you can stop your car to trigger your diametrically opposed pursuers into getting out of their vehicles and killing each other. Look for the entrance to the Yardie hideout, which is mostly blocked by a blue car up on blocks.

START ◯ Chinatown   **FINISH** ◯ Yardie Drug Factory

You can ride to Holywell Street in style, but you'll have to shoot it out with Triads for the privilege.

Let the rozzers and the Triads kill each other, while you make your way to the Yardie hideout.

A When you reach the Yardie hideout, four Triad cars appear--two on either side of you. Blast the drivers if you want, or simply run into the hideout. There's usually (but not always) a Yardie at the entrance with his back to you. Blast him and take his AK-47.

B As you enter the hideout, a flood of Triads pours through the entrance behind you. Fighting them all is suicide. Instead, turn to the right and run behind the shipping container, then crouch behind the wrecked car (after aiming to the left and shooting the shotgun-toting Triad who pursues you toward your hiding place). There's an AK-47 near the car if you need it.

C Peek around the car and take shots at whoever's closest to you, but mostly let the Yardies and Triads kill each other. Shoot the red barrel to blow up the Yardie sniper in the building.

D When all the Triads are dead, walk toward the Yardie building and kill the snipers in the windows, then shoot the shotgun-armed Yardie inside, who's the last witness to your presence here. Run back out to the street to complete the mission.

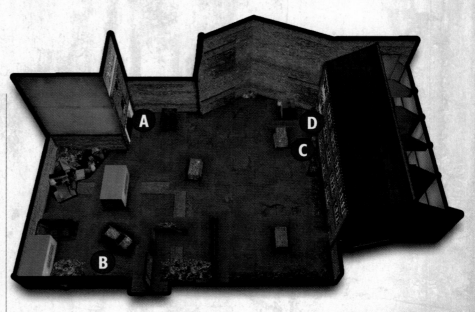

DRUG FACTORY
GROUND

Once you walk through this entrance into the courtyard, all hell will officially break loose.

Run away from the invading Triad army and shoot the persistent thug from your hiding place.

Use the power of manual aim to fire at the barrels near the door and the snipers in the windows

WALKTHROUGH

WALKTHROUGH

LONDON

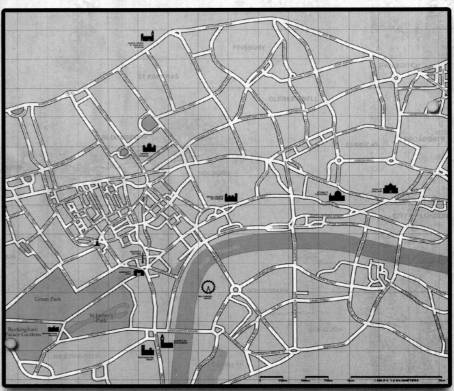

Y ou start the mission in front of the Yardie hideout, as the filth arrives on the scene. Boost the purple or green Civic and start driving toward the far-away Grosvenor Place. Now that you've "introduced" yourself to the Yardies, they'll chase you down in dark blue Rovers.

① During your long drive across London--expect to steal at least two or three cars along the way, as you leave wrecked ones behind, You'll also receive drive-by visits from the Triads and Soho boys, along with non-stop harassment from the filth.

② Look for the van on the sidewalk side of the street, It might be hidden from view behind a double-decker bus, so watch your turn signals to know for sure when you've found it. Get into the van to complete the mission.

START ◯ Yardie Drug Factory   **FINISH** ◯ Repair Van

Start

①

①
After the Holywell Street Massacre, you're at the top of yet another Most Wanted List.

②
The repair van is, on frequent occasion, cleverly concealed behind a double-decker bus. Be not fooled!

LONDON

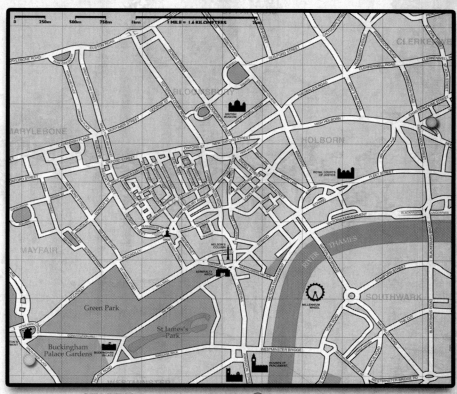

START ⦿ Repair Van   **FINISH** ⦿ Snow Hill Police Station

① At the start of the mission, you have eight minutes to track down the real repair van, which is parked curbside next to an HMV store. This is an overabundance of time, as it shouldn't take you much more than two minutes to find it.

② When you spot the van, it pulls out into traffic; you now have two minutes to disable it before it escapes. Take out the repair van by pulling up alongside it, then swerving and ramming it from the side. Keep whacking the van until the driver hits the brakes and bails out.

③ Once the van is disabled, you have all the time in the world to drive to the nearby Snow Hill. Pull up to the curb, get out, and walk inside.

①

②

③

①

②

You have two precious minutes to convince the driver of the repair van to take the day off.

③

Park in front of Snow Hill Police Station, take a deep breath, and enter the belly of the beast.

A As you enter the station, you're greeted by an officer. Follow him to the room with the phone lines, at which point he leaves you to your work. Thanks, rozzer.

B Backtrack to the blue corridor, where a sign on the wall points left to the first-floor stairs. Run down the hallway to the stairs and climb up. From this point on, you can't let yourself be seen by the cops, or you'll be arrested and/or shot, both of which bring the mission to a swift end.

C On the first floor, walk past the Intel Office to the intersection, then go down the right-hand corridor. Use the signs on the wall and turn around two more right-hand corners to find the Evidence Room. (You can stop at each office along the way to eavesdrop on the copper conversations.)

Allow the clueless rozzer to escort you into the building, then embark on a little unsupervised exploration.

D Inside the Evidence Room is a pistol on the floor. Take it, stash it by pressing TRIANGLE, and return to the hallway. Around the corner to the right is McCormack. Press yourself against the wall and wait for McCormack and his Kevlar-suited bodyguard to start walking.

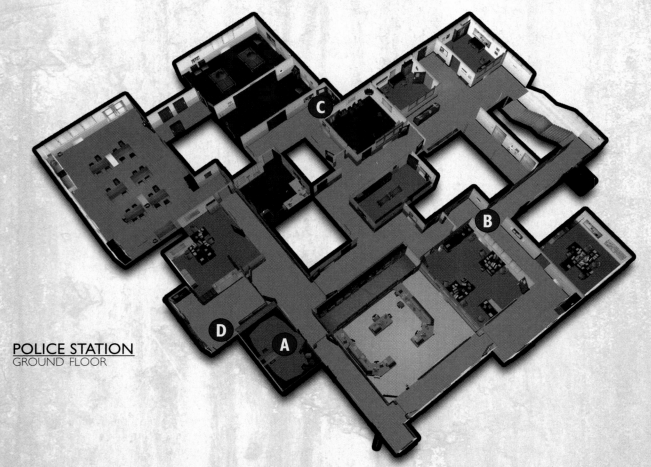

POLICE STATION
GROUND FLOOR

WALKTHROUGH

POLICE STATION
FIRST FLOOR

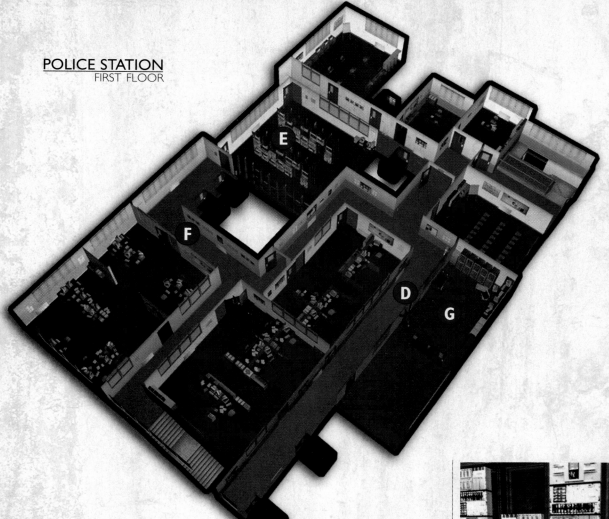

Stay against the wall and wait for McCormack to briefly pause at the adjacent office, then start moving again. Now you can follow him at a very respectful distance. If you get too close, McCormack bolts, alarms go off, police officers start shooting at you.

E In the Computer Room, McCormack parts ways with his arse-kissing bodyguard. Run around the far side of the room to avoid being seen by the brown-nosing rozzer. (If you try to kill him, you'll alert McCormack to your presence.)

F McCormack takes a detour through the Serious Fraud Squad office. You obviously can't follow him inside, so press up against the wall to the left of the door. When McCormack starts walking again, go left and wait for him to re-enter the hall-way, then continue your stalking ways.

G McCormack descends to the ground floor and makes his way to Interview Room 1. Follow him into the darkened office, pull your pistol, and shoot or pistol-whip him to death.

Run to the other side of the Computer Room to avoid the unpleasant end of the brown-nosing session.

McCormack can't be killed until you corner him in the Interview Room.

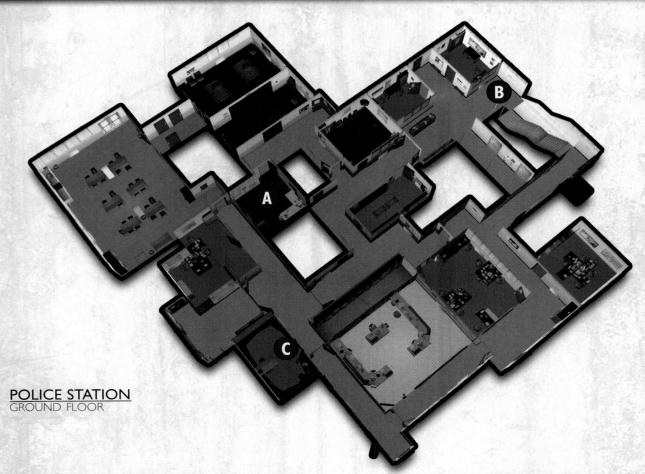

POLICE STATION
GROUND FLOOR

A Yasmin's on your side, and will shoot and pistol-whip cops whenever she sees them. Be careful you don't accidentally shoot her yourself, or she'll turn on you in an instant. From the interview room, head back toward the room with the phone lines.

B As you proceed toward the phone-line room, the rozzers fire a tear-gas grenade into the station. Round the corner, kill the gas-masked coppers, and take their MP5s. Now you're playing with power!

C In the final hallway before the phone-line room, instead of turning left, turn right and walk out into the parking lot. Your only route of escape now is the way you came in.

WALKTHROUGH

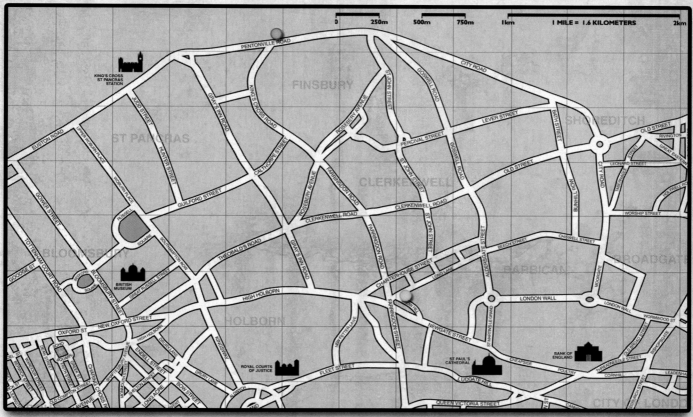

LONDON

START ● Snow Hill Police Station   **FINISH** ● Charlie's Depot

D Kill the gas-maskers at the reception desk, take their MP5s, and run outside. Boost the police car and head for Charlie's depot, which is at the top of a T intersection, with two white trucks parked in front. Run through the gate to complete the mission.

The parking lot in the rear of Snow Hill Police Station seems the perfect avenue of escape....

Yasmin covers you whenever you take respite against a wall. Hide around a corner and stay out of her way.

You'll never be deadlier in *The Getaway* than when you're packing twin MP5s, stolen from a cop's fresh corpse.

....until the door slams shut to prevent your escape. Time to head out the way you came in.

Enter the parking lot of Charlie's depot in a car or on foot. And bring a weapon with you.

WALKTHROUGH

LONDON

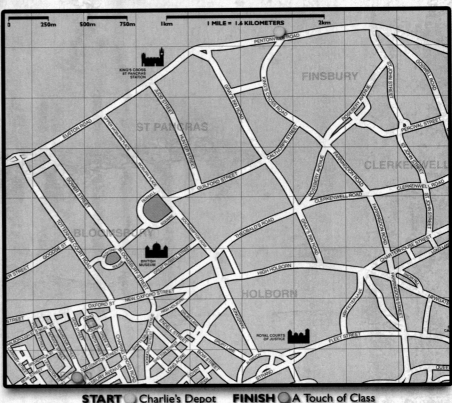

START ○ Charlie's Depot   **FINISH** ○ A Touch of Class

You start the mission in a speedy gray vehicle. Head for Soho, and take your time (if you want to avoid police attention) or violate all known traffic laws (if you want to quickly reach your destination). At one point, you'll likely pass through a police roadblock, but the foolish filth wave you through--if you're not running from them at the time, of course.

① Yasmin shoots out of the passenger side at any cops or gangsters who pull up alongside you, and she also defends you when you're boosting a car. Make sure you don't catch her in your crossfire, and make sure she doesn't get killed. Unlike you, she can't heal her wounds.

② There's a second police roadblock as you approach Soho, where the boys are waiting to give you a warm reception-- and by warm, we mean they try to shoot you dead. Look for A Touch of Class near a four-way intersection, with a pink neon sign and a doorman beckoning passersby to part with their pounds. Get out of the car and approach the nightclub.

You can drive like a nonce or a nutter, as long as you get to the nightclub with Yasmin.

Yasmin can't heal her wounds, and she refuses to take cover, so try to minimize her exposure to the rozzers.

Don't allow the cops to prevent you from savoring the sensual pleasures at A Touch of Class.

A Approach the doorman and he welcomes you into the club, even if you and Yasmin are filled with bullet holes and covered in blood. He's obviously been working here for a while. Enter the club and approach the stairs. Yasmin pops the doorman from behind, and the receptionist calls you names. (Alternately, you can just neck-break or pistol-whip the doorman as you enter.) Take the doorman's pistol if you need it, and proceed down the stairs.

B Move up against the left side of the doorway when you reach the bottom of the stairs and wait for a "dancer" to run past you. Lean around the corner and pick off the thug who runs at the doorway, then take out the distant thug who tries to hide behind a glass table.

C Move to the right side of the door way and manually aim at the thug behind the glass and the thug in the distance. Take them both out with head shots. Now move through the doorway and shoot the thug across the club, standing in front of the bar. Make sure to manually aim at his head, rather than relying on the auto-aim (which doesn't adjust for the railing in front of the thug).

Stay near the entrance, blast the patrons, and introduce a touch of evil to A Touch of Class.

D Proceed into the nightclub and turn left, walking past the private booths or through the stage area. A thug some-times attacks you from behind, but Yasmin takes care of him for you. A strip-per runs out of a booth on the right, fol-lowed by a thug; shoot the latter. Continue forward and take out two more thugs as you approach the bar.

E When you reach the bar, the bartender pops up from behind it and fires at you with an AK-47. Shoot back at him, running around the left side of the bar for a clear shot. Take his weapon when he drops. (Also, try shooting the

Explore the right-hand door for a fine weapon, then explore the left-hand door to complete the mission.

bottles on the bar to start a fire.

F There are two doors to the left of the bar. Go through the right-hand door and kill the AK-47-wielding thug, then go around and through the left-hand door, killing three more thugs. Walk toward the dancer next to the window to complete the mission.

NIGHTCLUB
BASEMENT

WALKTHROUGH

LONDON

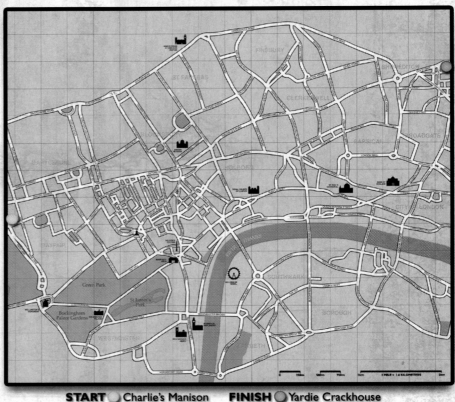

START ◯ Charlie's Manison   **FINISH** ◯ Yardie Crackhouse

You start the mission in a sleek Saab, with several Soho boys shooting at you and a Lexus pulling up behind you. Get out of the car and shoot the bad guys dead, then pick up the AK-47 of the terminated Lexus-driver if you need it (and steal his car, if you so prefer).

① Charlie's house isn't far from A Touch of Class. Stop in front of the open doorway, and Yasmin gets out.

② Now for the longer drive to the Yardie crackhouse. By this point, you should be used to constant harassment from the rozzers and the various gang members you've managed to piss off with your homicidal behavior.

③ The windows of the crackhouse are covered with green bars. Get out of the car and walk down the path on the left side of the crackhouse.

Start

②

①

Charlie's manse is a short drive from the nightclub. Drop Yasmin off in front and head off.

③

Nothing good can come out of your journey into the Yardie crackhouse. Make sure you bring a weapon.

A

B

C

A Move up against the corner and wait for one of the two Yardies to walk around the corner. Run up behind the first Yardie and break his neck, then continue to the second Yardie and repeat the brutal process. (Don't use a weapon to kill the first guard, or you'll alert the second.)

B Enter the crackhouse and shoot the Yardie sitting on the chair. This triggers a Yardie and his requisite crack-whore to emerge from the doorway on the right. Blast the Yardie, then shoot the whore if you don't feel like leaving any witnesses.

C Climb halfway up the stairs, then auto-aim and kill the Yardie inside the doorway on the left. This triggers a hatchet-wielding crack-whore to attack from the left. Two quick shots will take her out.

D Walk left and around the corner. There are three Yardies inside the second door on the right. (Sometimes, it's two, depending on whether or not one of

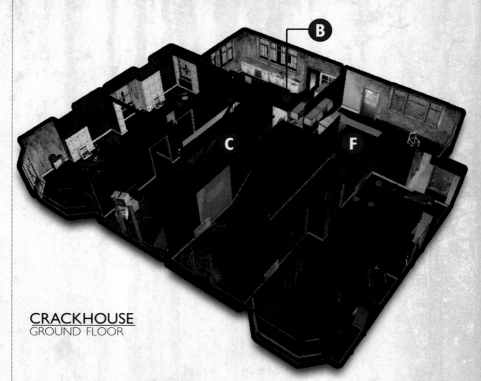

CRACKHOUSE
GROUND FLOOR

A

Yardie guards are often too busy practicing their incomprehensible slang to focus on the business of guarding.

B

The Yardie girl is unarmed, but the Yardie boy is packing heat. Kill him out of survival; kill her out of spite.

C

This Yardie gets a little crazy with the cutlery. Shoot her before she hacks off one or more of your limbs.

WALKTHROUGH

D

them comes downstairs when he hears the gunshots.) Go through the first door and shoot at the Yardies through the broken wall, which collapses from the impact of your bullets. When the Yardies are dead, silence their deafening tunes by shooting either turntable or both speakers.

E Return to the top of downward-leading staircase and go through the hole in the wall. Immediately auto-aim and kill the Yardie at the bottom of the staircase, then kill the pistol-packing Yardie who comes out of the doorway in front of you. Two (or three) more Yardies are behind the doorway to the right; at least one of them will come out to attack you.

F Go down the stairs and run into the dark room behind the staircase to find an AK-47 on the ground. Also take a moment to savor the Yardies' choice in

E

F

CRACKHOUSE
FIRST FLOOR

CRACKHOUSE
SECOND FLOOR

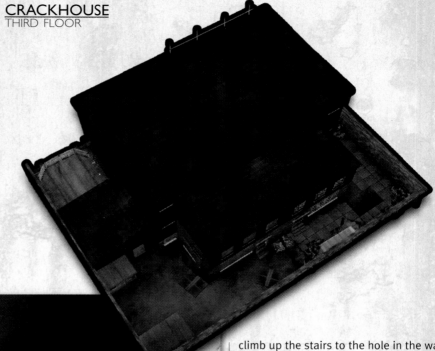

wall decoration. (Sometimes, there's a Yardie here, and other times, there isn't. If he's present, pistol-whip him with the quickness.)

G Return to the stairs and shoot two (or three) Yardies lying in wait, then

climb up the stairs to the hole in the wall, but don't go back through it. Instead, climb the next flight of stairs and kill four Yardies: two in the nearly doorway and two in the distance. (The two closer Yardies shoot at you as you ascend, and will probably hit you once or twice.)

H Enjoy the red-light room with the plethora of pinups on the walls, then return to the stairwell. Go through the holes in the wall and kill the Yardie on the other side. There's one more Yardie, carrying a shotgun, inside the doorway on the left. Kill him and walk up to the duffel-bag of cash on the table to complete the mission. (If the mission doesn't end, you haven't killed all the Yardies yet. Go downstairs and finish off the three or four stragglers, then come back upstairs and enter the money room again.)

You can't get your hands on the sackful of filthy lucre until you've disposed of all the Yardies.

WALKTHROUGH

WALKTHROUGH

LONDON

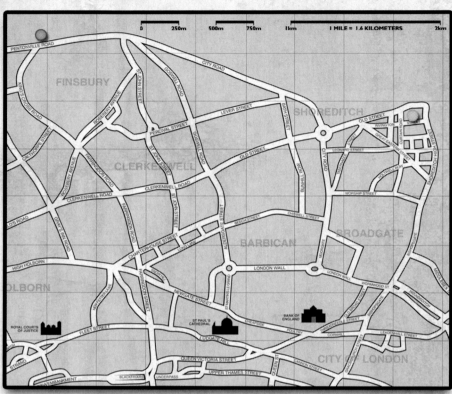

A t the start of the mission, a very angry Yardie runs at you with a baseball bat in his hand and murderous intentions on his mind. Blast him and quickly boost a car before more Yardies arrive at the scene.

(1) You'll be shocked--shocked!--to know that the filth will harass you during the long drive to the depot.

(2) You've been to Charlie's depot before, and you're going there again. Pull into the parking lot to complete the mission.

START ○ Yardie Crack House **FINISH** ○ Charlie's Depot

Start

(1)

Start

(2)

Give the Yardie a pistol-fueled anger-management lesson and take a car for the drive to the depot.

Charlie's depot has not moved since the last time you paid a visit, so finding it shouldn't be exceedingly difficult.

A

B

D

A Immediately move behind the stack of boxes and stay around the left side. Keep watching until Sparky, the crew member in the white sweater, walks toward you and turns to his left. Now move to the right side of the boxes and wait for Sparky to come around the corner. Quickly grab Sparky and break his maggot neck before he gets a shot off and brings the other thugs running. (It's much easier to kill Sparky this way than to shoot him, as he absorbs at least a dozen shots before dying.)

B Turn around and move toward the storage girders at the rear of the depot, hiding behind boxes and staying near the wall. Look for the ladder, climb up to the perch, and shoot the thug across from you when you reach the top.

C Turn right, move into the corner of the perch, and shoot the thug wandering around in the crates below. Take careful aim at the red crate in the middle of the warehouse and shoot it until it explodes, killing a couple of heavily armed thugs in the blast.

D Now for some trickier sniping. While still on your perch, take careful aim at the red box on the left side of the warehouse, behind the conveyor belt. Blast it until it explodes, killing a nearby thug.

E Go down the ladder across from the one you came up, then continue straight ahead and run through the "passage" in the girder. Stop as soon as you reach the other side, which protects you from the shotgun blasts of the thug behind the conveyor belt. (Take out a thug

CHARLIE'S DEPOT
GROUND FLOOR

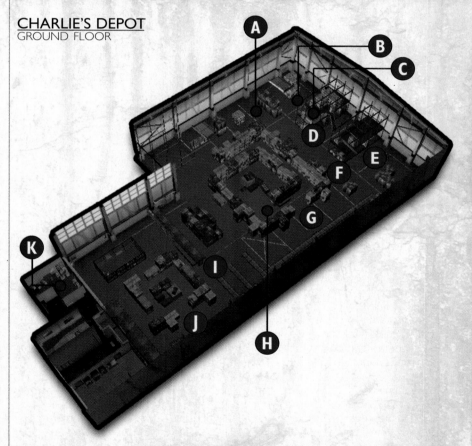

C

E

WALKTHROUGH

CHARLIE'S DEPOT
FIRST FLOOR

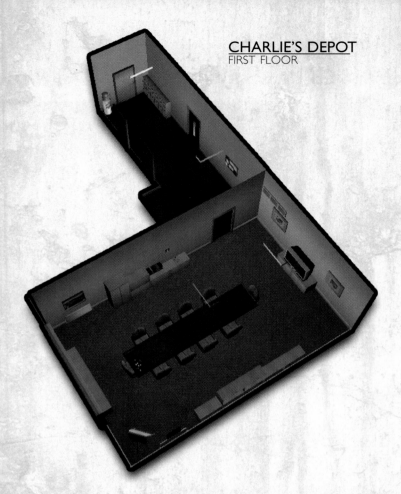

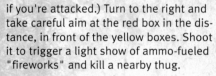

if you're attacked.) Turn to the right and take careful aim at the red box in the distance, in front of the yellow boxes. Shoot it to trigger a light show of ammo-fueled "fireworks" and kill a nearby thug.

F Move forward and shoot the yellow boxes behind the "fireworks," which causes a chain-reaction explosion at the other end of the depot.

G Move forward with the conveyor belt to your left. Shoot the thug in the distance, then turn right and shoot the thug standing in the "maze" of boxes (if he didn't already attack you earlier).

H Go into the "maze" and press up against the boxes to see a thug around the corner (he's not always there). As you see the first thug, a second thug usually attacks from behind you; quickly turn and shoot. Now kill the shotgun thug and grab an MP5 or shotgun from the ground.

I Return to the conveyor belt and run toward the staircase with Jake on it. Don't bother shooting at him, because you can't kill him. Take out a thug on the right, then hide behind the boxes and work your way toward the staircase to the left. A second thug usually attacks as you work your way toward the stairs. When you can see the stairs, Jake bolts through the upstairs door.

J Move toward the stairs. Climb up them and follow Jake. (If you're curious about the downstairs area, there's a shotgun-armed thug behind the soda machines, but nothing else.)

K Jake taunts you from the bottom of the stairwell and runs away. Descend the stairs and follow him through the depot's reception area. Enter the dark doorway at the end of the area to complete the mission.

The Getaway

Start

A

B

Let the divine Miss Yasmin do the heavy lifting at the start of the mission, then salvage an AK-47 from the aftermath.

Run out of the prison cell, and Yasmin blows away a trio of thugs. Grab two pistols from the floor and proceed around the corner, where Yasmin blasts several more wankers.

A Take the AK-47 from the cooling corpse and approach the stairs with Yasmin leading the way. Blast two more thugs (one of whom is armed with an MP5) and climb out of the basement.

Not that Yasmin's help isn't appreciated, but isn't it more enjoyable to take control of your destiny?

B Two groups of thugs attack as you reach the top of the stairs. Shoot both groups, then move toward the exit door. Don't wait here for long, or you'll be swarmed by more thugs.

C As you enter the next area, several more thugs attack. There's no subtlety required here. Shoot the thugs as quickly as you can, keep reloading, and take new pistols if your old ones run out of ammo.

The longer you stay in the warehouse, the longer the odds of getting out alive. Hurry to the door.

B

WALKTHROUGH

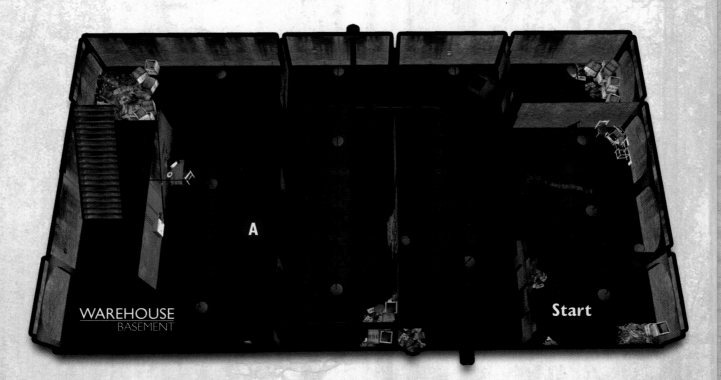

A

WAREHOUSE
BASEMENT

Start

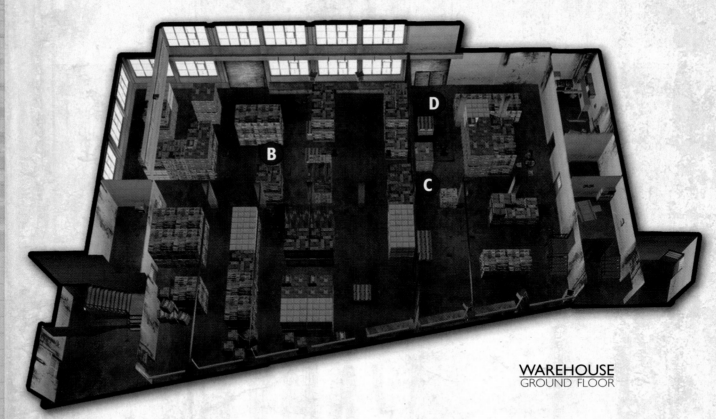

WAREHOUSE
GROUND FLOOR

D Turn left and break for the exit door. Shoot the thug behind the boxes near the door (who might be joined by a second baddie) and move forward. More thugs attack from behind as you reach the door, so quickly turn and shoot. Head outside and get into the white Lexus with quickness. Drive away from the warehouse in any direction until one of the turn signals comes on, which means you've completed the mission and moved onto the next.

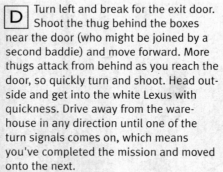

LONDON

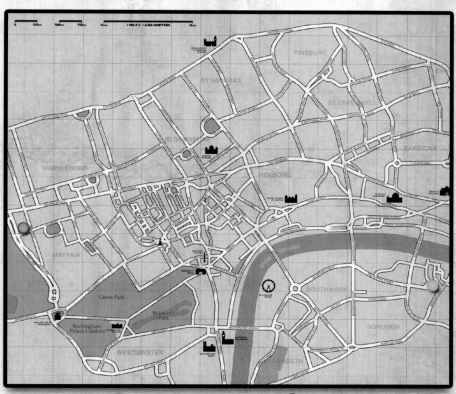

1. If you've been driving safely up until now, it's time to abandon that approach and start driving like a mad bastard. Keep the rozzers and various gang members far behind you.

2. When you reach Charlie's mansion, Yasmin gets out of the car and runs for the stairs to the left of the entrance. Get out of the vehicle and follow her down.

START ◯ Charlie's Warehouse   **FINISH** ◯ Charlie's Mansion

Everyone in London wants you dead, so it's time to dispense with the safe driving (if you haven't done so already).

Yasmin couldn't get through the security systems of Charlie's mansion. What makes you think you can do any better?

WALKTHROUGH

WALKTHROUGH

A

A Enter the basement of the mansion and follow Yasmin, who stops in front of a doorway. Walk through the doorway and a "wall" of lasers appears in front of you. Move up against either wall and sidestep past the wall. The lasers turn off as you step onto the invisible pressure pad on the other side. (You hear a click when you've touched the pad.)

B If you touch a laser beam, poisonous gas comes out of the small holes near the bottom of the walls, and an alarm summons any nearby thugs. If you're unlucky enough to stumble into one, get away from the gas as quickly as you can, and keep your back against a wall so you can see any approaching thugs.

C Proceed forward until lasers appear in the straight-ahead doorway. Go through the left-hand doorway into the kitchen, and neck-snap the cleaver-wielding thug before he screams and draws the attention of two nearby thugs. Run forward into the green-carpeted room and the lasers turn off.

B

CHARLIE'S MANSION
BASEMENT

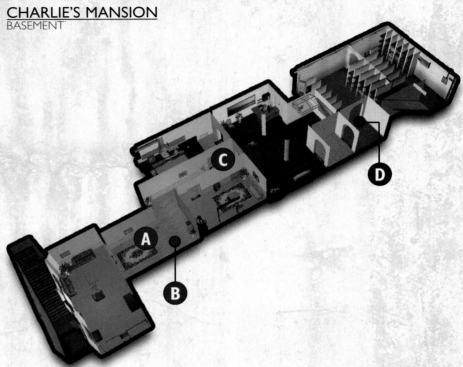

CHARLIE'S MANSION
GROUND FLOOR

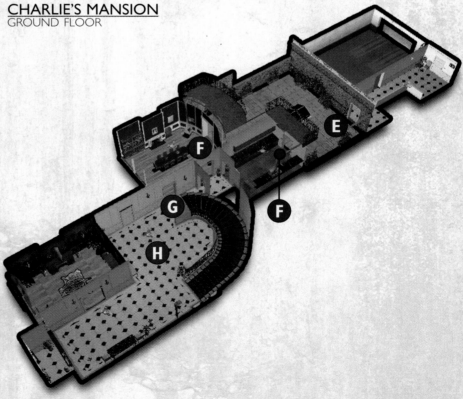

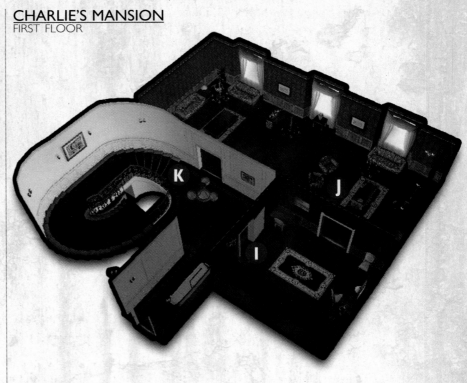

CHARLIE'S MANSION
FIRST FLOOR

D Proceed forward and move up against the left side of the archway. Eavesdrop on the two thugs, and end their conversation in a hailstorm of bullets. (If you got in a firefight with the kitchen thug, you already killed these thugs in the green room.) Continue forward to the staircase. You'll run into two thugs, one with a shotgun, if you spilled blood in the green room. Press up against the wall, and sidestep past the lasers until they turn off.

E Climb up the stairs and shoot two thugs through the doorway. One of them has a shotgun. Now move out to the courtyard and blast the thug behind the skylight. (There's a second thug on the balcony if you copped the thugs in the green room.)

CHARLIE'S MANSION
SECOND FLOOR

The first rule of bodyguarding: Don't stare out at a panoramic view when there's an armed ex-con running amok.

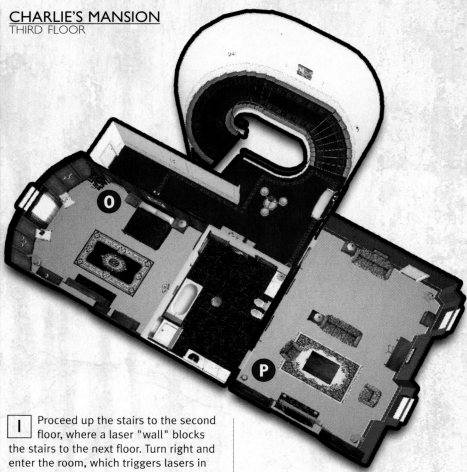

F Proceed through either of the two doors. When you do, lasers are activated in both of them, preventing Yasmin from following.

G Move down the dark corridor until a high "wall" of lasers appears in front of you. Press X + UP to roll underneath the lasers and trigger the pressure pad, which allows Yasmin to catch up to you.

H Turn left and shoot the thug as he descends the winding staircase, then shoot a second thug around the corner to the right. Pay a visit to Charlie's trophy room to trigger some chat between Mark and Yasmin.

I Proceed up the stairs to the second floor, where a laser "wall" blocks the stairs to the next floor. Turn right and enter the room, which triggers lasers in the doorway. Continue into the next room, which is criss-crossed with several grids of lasers.

J Face the far end of the room and roll under the high lasers, between the wall and the red chairs. Now turn right and roll under the single laser, into the wall. You'll automatically press up against it at the end of the roll. Sidestep to the left, past several lasers, and carefully step away from the wall.

K Return to the staircase to step on the pressure pad, and shoot the thug to your right. (Additional thugs might attack from the lower staircase.) Climb up to the third floor, where the stairs to the fourth floor are blocked by beams. Turn right and slowly enter the room; lasers appear in front of and behind you.

L Turn right, move up against the wall, and sidestep left, past several

Yasmin won't be able to help you on your journey through the laser maze of the mansion's first floor.

Roll under the laser beam, and you automatically move up against the wall in a "stealth" position.

Enter each room slowly to avoid stumbling into lasers that suddenly appear in front of you.

lasers. Move away from the wall and roll under the high lasers on the side of the pool table, then turn and roll under the high lasers on the other side of the pool table.

M Walk forward into the next room. Turn left and roll under the high laser, into the wall. (Aim for the spot between the table and the door.) Sidestep right to the door, which triggers the pressure plate.

N Move into the next room and roll under the high lasers. Return to the staircase, shoot the descending thugs, and climb to the next floor. Another wall of lasers impedes your progress; turn right and walk around the corner.

O Walk down the corridor and slowly enter the bedroom as lasers appear in front of and behind you. Roll forward under the high lasers. A thug appears in the doorway on the right side of the bed; manually aim and shoot him. Now roll under the lasers to the doorway.

P Walk through the bathroom and into the living room. Roll under the high lasers near the fireplace and turn left. Move toward the next doorway and roll under the high lasers. Return to the stairway and shoot the thugs. Climb the stairs to the highest floor of the mansion and enter the bedroom to complete the mission.

When you negotiate the security system on a particular floor, thugs march down the stairs from the floor above.

LONDON

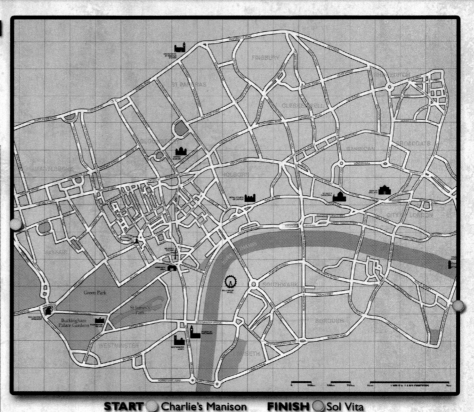

START ○ Charlie's Manison   **FINISH** ○ Sol Vita

Y ou start the mission outside Charlie's mansion, with several cop cars to your right (most of the time). Mow down the rozzers and boost the nearest vehicle, but make sure it's a quick one. After you boost a car, you have a limited amount of time to reach the Sol Vita.

① The rozzers and gang members are on you throughout the drive. If your car is banged up and slowed down, quickly boost another fast car. Don't get caught up in any time-wasting shoot-outs; hop into a car and keep driving.

② You can't drive directly to the Sol Vita, as all the roads leading to it are closed, but you'll eventually get close enough for Yasmin to make a comment. Look for the "No Through Road" sign, and the cones in the road. Drive through the cones to find an alleyway on the left. Get out of the car and run through the alleyway to find the Sol Vita at the other end.

Start

While you would normally delight in the simple pleasures of shooting rozzers and villains, you simply don't have the time.

①

②

②

The path to the Sol Vita is a roundabout one. Look for the traffic cones and the forboding sign.

WALKTHROUGH

SOL VITA
DECK

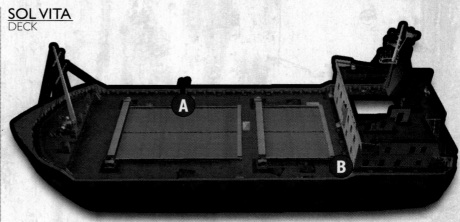

A Run to the opposite side of the ship, where Yasmin waits for you to politely escort her up the ramp and onto the ship. You arrive in the midst of a massive firefight, so feel free to join the party and shoot everyone on the deck, picking up shotguns and AK-47 from the cooling corpses as you see fit.

B Yasmin waits for you at the stairs on the right side of the ship. Follow behind her and take out a group of thugs as you climb up. Go around the corner, shoot several thugs on the opposite side of the deck, and enter the door to the left.

C At the top of the staircase, Yasmin wishes you luck. Descend into the engine room where you're shot by Harry on the way down the stairs. Climb to the bottom of the room and shoot two thugs hiding behind the turbine.

D Leave the engine room and turn left. Aim and shoot at the red barrels to kill a thug in the explosion. Quickly turn around and shoot the red barrels on the opposite side to flame broil several more baddies.

Harry nails you with a cheap shot as you descend into the engine room. He will regret his bastardly actions.

Blast the red barrels in the corridors to set off thug-immolating explosions.

SOL VITA
BRIDGE HOUSE QUARTERS

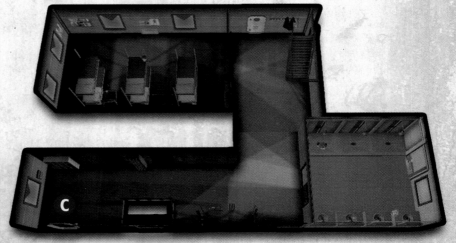

WALKTHROUGH

E

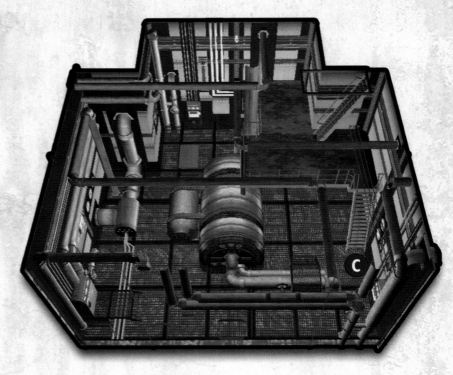

E Stay near the exit of the engine room and keep targeting and blasting thugs in either direction until they stop appearing. When the sheep stop volunteering for slaughter, turn to face the engine-room exit, then turn left and enter the long corridor. Immediately turn left and shoot the thugs behind the barrels (or the barrels themselves).

F Proceed forward and blast two thugs as they attack from around the corner. Lean around the corner and take out the thug on the railing above. You can shoot him directly, or blast the barrels below the railing.

G Continue forward and shoot several thugs in the corridor in front of you. Be careful of the thug on the right side of the corridor, who's well hidden behind the steel hold. Another thug might attack you from behind, so swing around and blast him as well.

H There's a door into the cargo hold on the left side of the corridor. Stand outside the door and wait until a crate smashes into the floor in front of you. At regular intervals, this crate rises into the air, maneuvers above your location in the hold, and smashes to the ground after a brief series of warning beeps. The only ways to avoid the crate are to keep moving, or to position yourself in areas of the

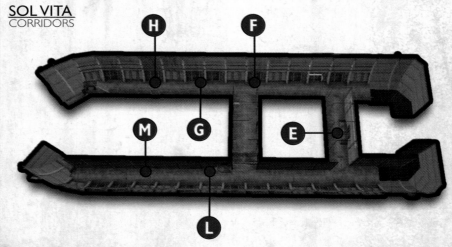

F

G

H

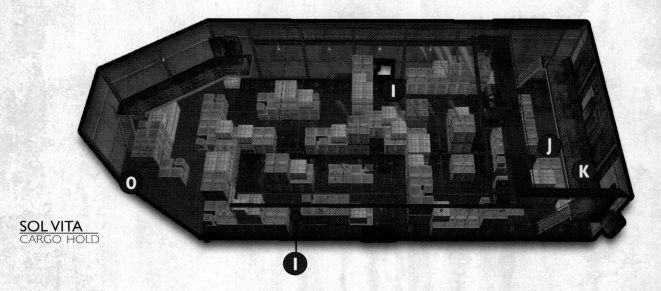

SOL VITA
CARGO HOLD

hold that the crate can't reach--the narrow alcoves between crates or the dark areas under the railings.

I From the cargo-hold entrance, run left and shoot the thug at the other end of the "aisle," then continue left and blast the thug on the railing above. Hide in the crate alcove if you need a rest.

J Move forward and turn left, following the path underneath the railing. Now turn left and climb the ladder against the wall.

K Harry's at the opposite end of the hold, and while you can target him, he's too far away to hit with a weapon. Run to the opposite end of the railing and shoot the thug in the doorway on the left, then go through the doorway directly ahead.

L Turn to the right and shoot the thug at the bottom of the stairs, then descend the stairs back into the corridor. Immediately turn around and shoot a group of thugs.

M Turn around again and run forward to a door on the right, leading into the cargo hold. Wait at the door until a forklift drives into view. Shoot the driver until he slumps over, or blast the propane tank on the back of the 'lift.

N Proceed into the hold and head for the railing with Harry cowering behind a crate. Make your way through the maze of crates, shooting thugs and hiding in narrow alcoves to rest. Don't shoot it out with Harry, as you can't kill him just yet.

O Move under the railing and work your way around to the ladder. Climb up and shoot the now-vulnerable Harry until the bastard stops moving.

You can target Harry from the Cargo Hold floor.

Start

A

Wait for the punk to draw his piece before you take him out, so that you can take it for yourself.

B

This is a dead-end as the staircase collapses as you approach.

Follow your partner into the brothel. After waiting for you to catch up, he sprints down the right-hand corridor. While you can follow him, all you'll find is a collapsing stairway, so head left instead.

A There are two thugs around the first corner. The first is armed, so shoot him without remorse and take his pistol (which won't drop the ground unless he's drawn it first). The second is just an unfortunate john, so shoot him or arrest him X to grab, SQUARE to hog-tie as you choose.

B Proceed down the hallway and turn left at the "Lift/Stairs" sign. Approach the staircase and it collapses to the floor. Guess we won't be going that way then. Return to the sign, turn left, and continue down the hall.

C As you approach the corner, the wall on the left side of the hallway is destroyed by a shotgun blast. Turn left and shoot the thug, but try not to kill the harmless prostitute in the crossfire. Continue around the corner and blast two thugs to the right, standing below the hole in the ceiling.

D Take the shotgun from the thug you caught in flagrante delicto, then backtrack and move down the hallway with the hole. Pause underneath the hole, wait for a patrolling thug to walk into your point of view, and fill him with buckshot.

E Continue down the hallway and climb the stairs to the first floor. Blast a thug at the top of the staircase and walk forward, then turn left and kill a thug as he comes out of the doorway.

C

D

WALKTHROUGH

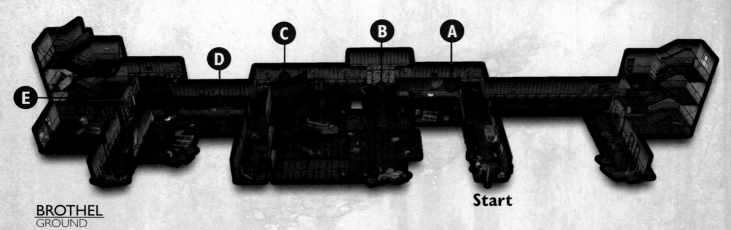

E   D   C   B   A

Start

BROTHEL
GROUND

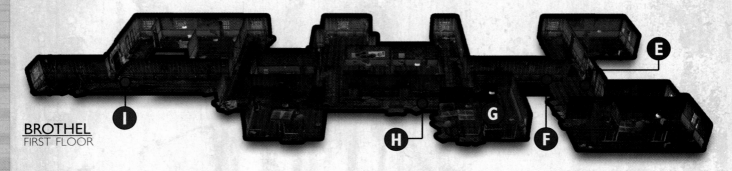

BROTHEL
FIRST FLOOR

F Move against the wall on the right side of the hole in the hallway and sidestep left to the other side. Do not press X to move away from the wall until you're safely on the other side, or you'll plunge to a very embarrassing death.

G On the other side of the hole, go into the doorway to find a dirty transaction in progress. Return to the hallway, then run left and around the corner, blasting two thugs down the corridor.

H Walk down the hallway and blast the thug who comes out of the right-hand doorway. Continue down the hallway and shoot two more thugs hiding inside the left-hand doorway. Now move forward until the left-hand wall explodes, then

turn and shoot the shotgun thug inside the hole.

I Continue down the hallway, turning right and then left. Move against the wall and sidestep across the hole. Run down the aisle and kill the thug inside the doorway, then return to the stairway and climb to the second floor.

J At the top of the stairs, immediately turn right and blast two thugs. Walk into the hallway and a group of policemen storm past you into the building. Proceed down the hall, allowing your teammates' MP5s to take care of the bad guys.

K Continue down the hallway and kill a thug inside the doorway on the right. Move forward and kill a thug in the hallway to the left (the one leading to the lift). Continue to the end of the hallway, where the coppers are waiting for you.

L Head around the corner and a couple of cops fall through a section of the fragile floor. Move up against the wall and sidestep across the hole. Go left around the corner and into the room, where your backup forces arrest Jake, completing the mission.

BROTHEL
SECOND FLOOR

LONDON

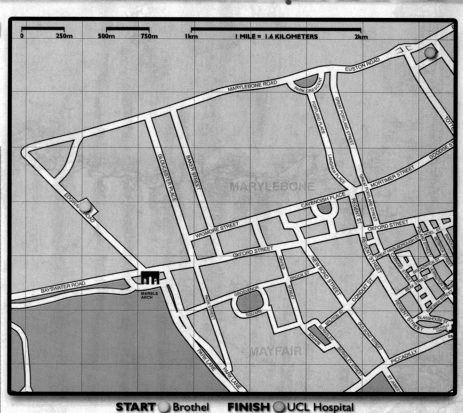

(1) You have two and a half minutes of real-time to drive from the brothel to the hospital. Instead of taking the unmarked gray car in which you started the mission, take one of the police cars on the scene. Several roadblocks will be set up along the route to the hospital.

(2) Press L3 to turn on the siren, which causes most of the traffic to pull over to the side of the road as you approach. It's easier to drive fast when you're not quite so concerned with getting into a head-on collision. If you do get into an engine-wrecking smash-up, you'll never reach the hospital in time.

(3) Look for the blue signs at roadside and follow them to the entrance of UCL. Pull up to the entrance of UCL to complete the mission.

START ○ Brothel   **FINISH** ○ UCL Hospital

Pile into a police car and turn on the siren to give yourself a much easier journey to UCL.

You have to drive flawlessly to reach the hospital before Joe bleeds out. Better to hit the brakes then get into a head-on.

WALKTHROUGH

LONDON

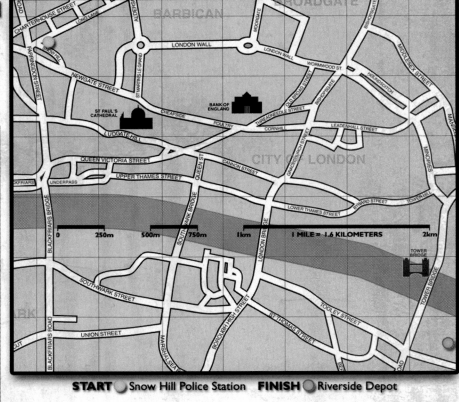

START ◯ Snow Hill Police Station **FINISH** ◯ Riverside Depot

Y ou start in the parking lot of Snow Hill Police Station, driving an unmarked vehicle. Fortunately, you don't need drive like a civilian; you can ram into cop cars, steal civilian cars, and run over civilians without any negative consequences. Ah, the joys of Flying Squad membership.

On your way to the depot, you'll be harassed by Yardies. Pull over and blast them, or simply continue toward your destination. Look for a wide gate and follow the road to a gate on the right side, with a stack of multicolored shipping containers nearby.

Start

Start

You can boost any motor you see without risking the wrath of the police, since you ARE the police.

The Yardies will do what they can to keep you away from the depot, but DC Carter is not easily dissuaded from anything.

A Approach the gate and uphold the law on a posse of Yardies who turn and scatter. Proceed into the depot and shoot down a sniper on the shipping containers above the gate.

B Each row of shipping containers in the depot is being constantly circled by a huge yellow crane. This crane crushes you (and any Yardies foolish enough to get in its way) upon impact. There are gaps in most of the container rows where you can safety wait for a crane to roll past you. Use these gaps as you proceed into the depot.

C Negotiate the cranes, blasting any Yardies you encounter along the way. When you see two giant spools, you've made it through the first section of the maze.

D There are many more Yardies in the second section of the depot, and you can kill as few or as many of them as you want. Your only objective is to find the

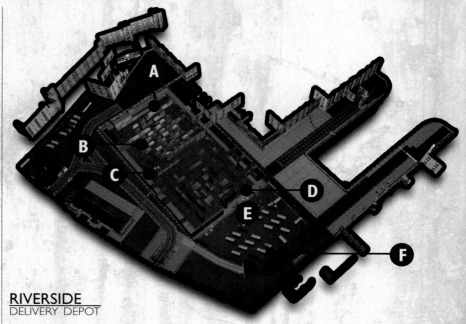

RIVERSIDE
DELIVERY DEPOT

white van in the parking lot, which pulls away as you approach.

E There are dozens of Yardies in the lot, and you'll be smoked if you charge into them. Wait for your fellow officers to arrive and exchange fire with the Yardies, then move into the lot. If an officer is cut down, take his MP5; you can carry two of them.

F The van is at the back of the lot, behind one of the trailers. Walk up to the van to complete the mission.

The white van is cleverly parked out of sight behind the truck trailer.

Make your way through the maze of containers, dodging cranes and blasting Yardies. (The latter is more enjoyable.)

As you approach the white van, it screeches to the other end of the parking lot. Head off in pursuit.

Take AK-47s off the fallen cops and use them to cut a swath through the remainder of the Yardies.

WALKTHROUGH

LONDON

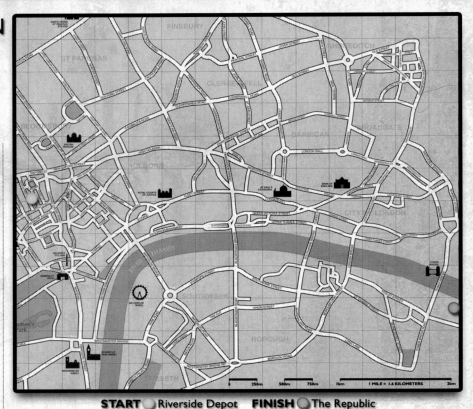

START ● Riverside Depot   **FINISH** ● The Republic

Y ou have four and a half minutes of real-time to drive from the depot to The Republic restaurant in Soho, not an easy feat. Fortunately, your unmarked car is equipped with a police siren, which easily parts traffic. It also attracts the attention of Soho boys, who ram and shoot at your car with great vengeance and furious anger.

Most of the drive to The Republic will be either the wrong way on a one-way street or through the middle of two-way traffic. It can't be helped; you need to take the straightest route to Soho, and that's against the grain. If (when) you smash your police car, steal a speedy replacement. (The longer you can keep your police car intact, the better.) When you reach any of the police road-blocks near The Republic, get out of your vehicle and run toward the smoke.

Press L3 to turn on your police siren during the mad dash to The Republic.

But be prepared for frequent attacks by the Soho boys as you enter their turf.

If the police car's siren is knocked out and black smoke is pouring out of the hood, it's time to boost a speedy vehicle.

A

A

B

A Move toward the restaurant, and a few cops come along with you. Auto-aim with R1 to target rioting Soho boys in the thick smoke. Continue down the street and blast a couple of boys behind the Lexus.

B March forward and unleash hell on the Soho boys as they move within range of your pistols. Near the end of the street, several Soho cars skid onto the scene. Finish off the boys inside them, then take out the crowd of criminals in the square to complete the mission.

B

C For some crime-stopping variety, you can drive your car around the police roadblocks and run over the rioters, but they'll quickly shoot out your tires and your windows, then kill you inside your car. If you're going to try this approach, make sure you have a sturdy vehicle--such as, a fire truck...

C

B

Boost a fire truck and see how many Soho boys you can hit-and-run before they blow you up.

March down the street and frag each Soho boy as he gets within range. Pistols are better than the AK-47 in this instance.

LONDON

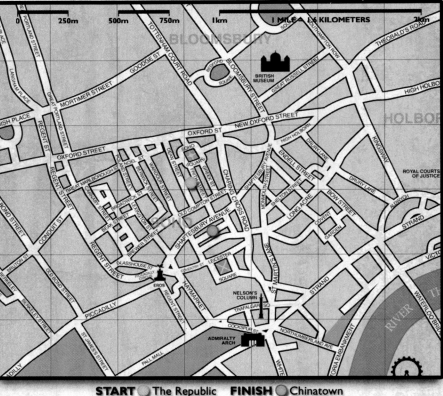

START ○ The Republic   FINISH ○ Chinatown

You have four and a half minutes of real-time to drive from Soho to Chinatown, but this is a much shorter and easier drive than the one in Mission 15. Once again, you're sporting an unmarked car with a police siren, which makes your drive slightly easier. You shouldn't even encounter any gang members during the short journey.

① You can enter the main drag of Chinatown on foot or in a car, shooting or smashing into the Yardies and Triads to thin them out. Head all the way down the drag, spilling claret as you go.

② There's a parking garage at the end of the drag. Go inside to enter the second phase of the mission.

③ And now for a dirty little secret. You don't really have to kill all the gangsters in Chinatown. If you prefer, just drive your car all the way down the drag (avoiding the burned-out wrecks) and into the car park to reach the second phase.

Drive onto the main drag and run over everyone with a gun--which is everyone in Chinatown.

If you smash into one of the wrecks or you're getting shot to hell, bail out of the car and proceed on foot.

Get into the NCP Carpark after killing all the Triads or simply driving past (and over) them.

NCP CARPARK
GROUND FLOOR

You'll have a police escort for the first half of the mission, but he may very well go down. (in which case, take his MP5!)

Take out the Triads as they peer over the smoking wreckage, then boost the tireless car for a good laugh.

A Make your way down to the first level where Yardies and Triads are exchanging fire. If you've brought a car down here, your goal is simply to run over anyone who's moving on both the first and second basement levels. (You'll have to enter the third level on foot.)

B If you're entering the first level on foot, approach the firefight with both guns blazing. Most of the Yardies and Triads will be too busy shooting each other to notice you. A cop escorts you on your explorations, although he might well be killed for his troubles.

C Move forward, past the smoking wreckage, and continue thinning out the bad guys. For a nice laugh, get into the purple car with no tires, just past the two wrecks, and take a "drive." The cop escort even gets into the car with you!

If you bring a car into the NCP (or boost one inside), run over Triads and Yardies with reckless abandon.

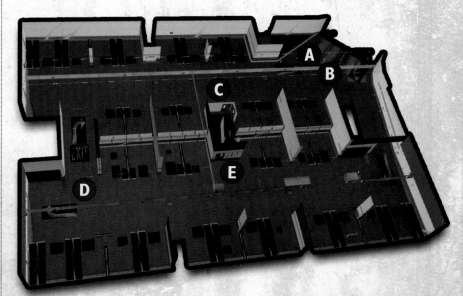

NCP CARPARK
BASEMENT ONE

WALKTHROUGH

D. Walk down the ramp to the next level; three Triads charge down ahead of you. Move forward and take out the Triads from long range. (Use pistols or an MP5.) You can get into the green car to the left and use it to ram the Triads for extra-violent fun. When you need a break, position yourself so that the escort is shooting the bad guys while you're healing your wounds.

E. As you approach the ramp to the next level, a Yardie car smashes into the wall and brings the air-conditioning pipes crashing down. Shoot the driver when he gets out, then turn around and go down the staircase.

F. Charge out of the doorway and you're followed by a flood of officers. Turn left and approach the parked cars; two of them zoom down the ramp to the next level. Turn around and finish off the gangsters on the level (if the cops haven't done it for you), then pursue the cars downward. Take the parked black Nissan, or continue to hoof it.

G. Blast all the Triads on this otherwise uneventful level and walk down the

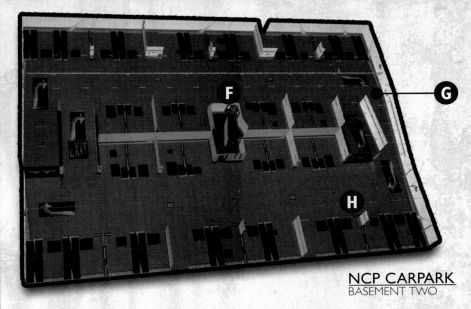

NCP CARPARK
BASEMENT TWO

ramp on the left side. Hide behind the walls if you're taking a lot of fire.

H. You'll see several parked cars in the stalls. Approach them while staying on the left side of the level (opposite the purple car). As you get close, the purple car suddenly jets down the right side of the lever, and several Triads attack. Shoot them all and descend to the next level, either on foot or in a Triad car. (We suggest the latter.)

I. There are two parked cars in the middle of this lowest (and final) level of the car park, and a dozen Triads shooting at you. Several coppers charge the ramp behind you to provide backup, so shoot-and-reload or hit-and-run until you've killed every Triad and completed the mission.

A combination of police MP5s and hit-and-run tactics will make quick work of the Triads at the bottom of the carpark.

NCP CARPARK
BASEMENT THREE

LONDON

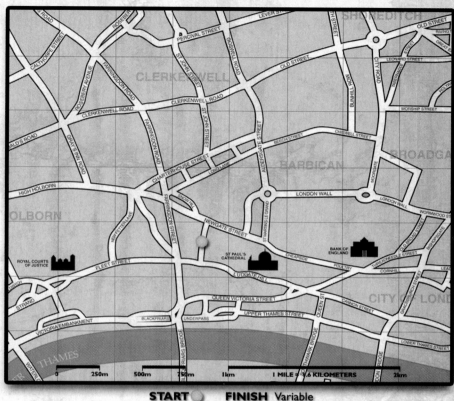

START ●   **FINISH** Variable

After the convoy is attacked, you're given two and a half minutes of real-time to take out a silver Range Rover. Immediately press L3 to turn on your siren or don't; it seems to make very little difference in this mission.

① The Range Rover's driver is exceptionally skilled, weaving through traffic and making sharp turns to try to ditch you. If you lose sight of the Rover, you'll have a very hard time catching up. If you get into an accident, you'll probably never catch up. You have to drive almost flawlessly if you're going to take the Rover off the road--no ramming into other cars and no switching vehicles. The good news is the Rover drives the same path every time, so if you fail on your first attempt,

you'll know when and where he turns on your second.

② There are only a few points during the chase where you can catch up to the Rover, such as inside the tunnel and You have to capitalize on these moments. Pull alongside the Rover and smash into it from the side to cause damage. If you're lucky, you can disable the Rover with a single attack, but you'll probably need to smash it at least twice. You know you've done damage with a ramming attack if the Rover starts emitting black smoke.

③ When the Rover is disabled, kill the occupants to complete the mission.

Start

①

The Range Rover strikes hard and fast, and you'll be very fortunate not to lose sight of it.

②

③

Ram the Range Rover from the side until its driver and passenger are immolated by the flames of their burning vehicle.

LONDON

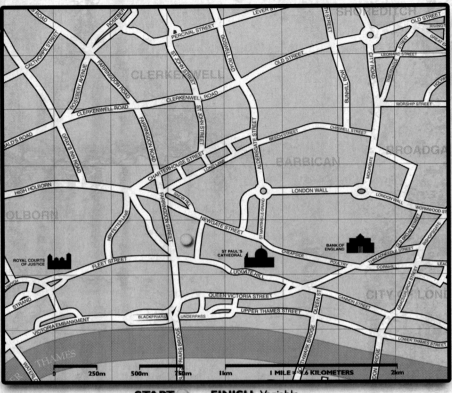

START ⚪   FINISH Variable

① If you're doing this mission immediately after the previous one you're in your wrecked-up vehicle; boost a faster car in better shape. If you're starting this mission in an intact police vehicle, just turn on the siren and hit the gas. You have two and a half minutes of real-time to catch up to the convoy.

② Drive straight ahead toward the convoy. If you're passing wrecked cars, you know you're headed in the right direction. You won't actually see the convoy when you catch up to it. Just keep following the turn signals and driving as fast as you can. When the screen fades out, you've completed the mission.

Steal a car if your current vehicle is wrecked, or stay inside the police car if you're starting the mission over.

Watch for wrecked cars to know you're headed in the direction of the convoy (which you won't see during the mission).

LONDON

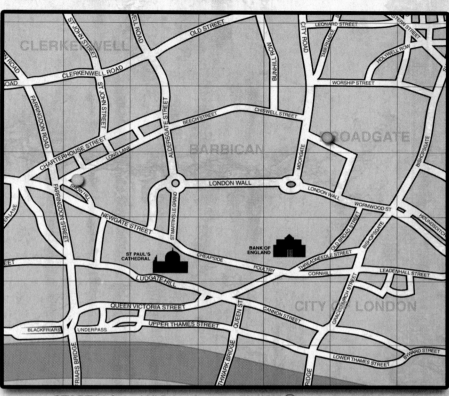

Y ou have two and a half minutes to get from Snow Hill to the front "entrance" of the Yardie drug factory. You start the mission in your decidedly unglamorous automobile, so abuse your police privilege and boost a faster car on the street outside the Snow Hill parking lot. Head right from the parking lot for the quickest route to the factory.

1 As you approach the entrance (with two pistol-packing Yardies in front), a couple of Yardies ram you from behind to try to stop you, but surely you can handle the thugs. Run over the Yardie guards and run down the alleyway to the factory.

2 Make sure you don't accidentally turn left and try to enter the factory from the rear entrance (with the blue car on blocks), which leads to a dead end.

START ◯ Snow Hill Police Station **FINISH** ◯ Yardie Drug Factory

You start the mission in a wretched car. Boost a better one immediately, then make your way into Yardie territory.

Don't turn left. Instead, go straight ahead and look for a Yardie guard posted at the entrance of the alleyway.

WALKTHROUGH

A Run down the alleyway and shoot the two Yardies in front of the door, then a third Yardie who pops out of the entrance to attack. (Another Yardie or two might come up behind you, so be ready.)

B Enter the factory and climb the stairs to the first floor. (A Yardie might attack from behind as you're about to climb up, but this is rare.) At the top of the stairs, two Yardies attack: one from the left and one from the hydroponics room. Immediately shoot the one on the left and press up against the wall, then lean to the right and shoot each Yardie as he appears in the doorway.

C Rest against the wall, then run into the hydroponics room. Take the AK-47 from one of the dead Yardies, and shoot three bad guys: one behind the turntable on the left and two behind the plants. You can silence the music by shooting either of the turntables of both of the speakers. Whew.

D Return to the hallway and climb up the stairs to the second floor. Move up against the wall to the left of the door-way and peek inside at the "manufacturers." Lean into the doorway and shoot the red propane tank on the floor, which causes an explosion and sets several Yardies ablaze. Three Yardies run through the door to attack; shoot or pistol-whip each one as he comes through.

B

The Yardies are very protective of their hydroponic technology, but they should be more worried about their lives.

C

If drum-and-bass music isn't your thing, put a bullet in the turntables to proceed in blessed silence.

B

Hide behind the wall and let the Yardies run down the hallway to their foolish demises.

D

Shoot the propane tank to destroy the table and kill a few Yardies, leaving you several more to mop up.

DRUG FACTORY
GROUND FLOOR

A

This Yardie isn't a particularly skilled guard, but his peculiar patois is always good for a laugh.

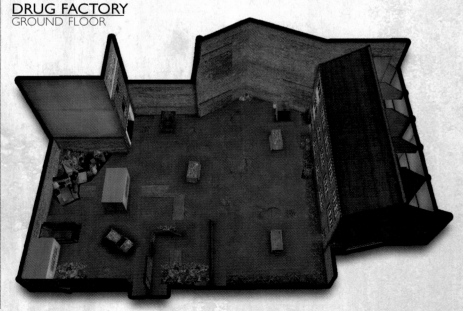

E Stay against the wall and lean into the doorway to snipe each Yardie inside the room. Move away from the wall to rest, then move up against the wall to resume sniping. When you've picked off all the Yardies, carefully move through the doorway so as to avoid setting yourself on fire. Run through the door on the other side of the room to complete the mission.

Play with fire and you're going to get burned, so stay as far from the flames as possible when you walk through the doorway.

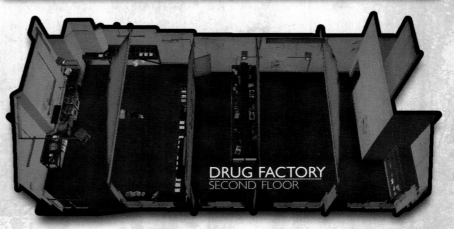

DRUG FACTORY
SECOND FLOOR

WALKTHROUGH

WALKTHROUGH

LONDON

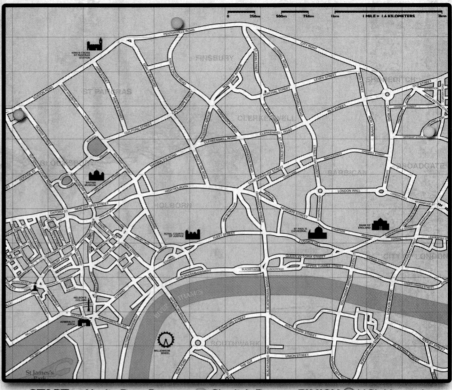

START ○ Yardie Drug Factory   ○ Charlie's Depot   **FINISH** ○ UCL Hospital

Y ou start the mission on the second floor of the drug factory. Make your way to the ground floor, once again taking care not to set yourself ablaze. You don't have to wait for your gimpy companions, so forge ahead without them. Shoot the Yardies just inside (or outside) the door to the courtyard, then go through the right-hand door and run into the alley.

① There are two Yardies in the alley; shoot them both and run out to the street. A Yardie car and a cop car pull up at the same time. You probably know who to shoot. Take the Yardie AK-47, and boost the Yardie vehicle.

② As you reach Snow Hill, McCormack pulls out of the parking lot ahead of you, and Carter makes a comment. Follow McCormack's dark red vehicle, but not too closely. If your hazard lights come on, you're tailing too close--and McCormack will soon spot you, which prematurely ends the mission. If you're following in a police car, don't run the siren--that tends to draw attention. Just stay at a reasonable distance with McCormack barely visible in the distance, and rely on your turn signals.

③ McCormack pulls into the parking lot of a depot with several trucks outside. Enter the parking lot behind him and watch as he enters the building. Get out of your car and follow him.

Start

②

①

③

Shoot a Yardie outside the courtyard door, but don't wander into the warzone; leave through the alley instead.

Give McCormack a wide berth as he drives to the depot; watch your hazard lights to make sure you're not too close.

A Follow McCormack into the depot and through the reception area. When you reach the inside of the depot, press up against the crates on the right. Listen to McCormack converse with the thug, then wait as they start walking toward the middle of the depot. Follow behind them.

B Move up against the yellow brick wall and listen as one thug commands another. When the two of them start walking away, move around the corner, turn left, and run behind the boxes. Press up against them and wait until a thug walks past you. Run up behind him and apply a hog-tie (press X to grab him, then SQUARE).

C Head for the other end of the row of boxes and walk around the corner. Run over to the wall and stay against it as you run to the back of the depot. At one point, you'll see McCormack and several thugs in the distance, but they won't see you as long as you don't approach them.

D Keep moving to the back of the depot until you see a ladder. Climb the ladder and look down as McCormack walks away.

CHARLIE'S DEPOT
GROUND FLOOR

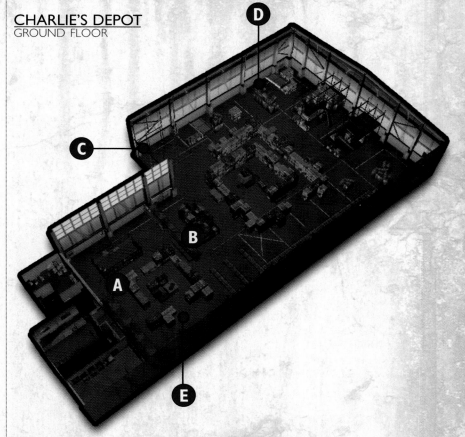

CHARLIE'S DEPOT
FIRST FLOOR

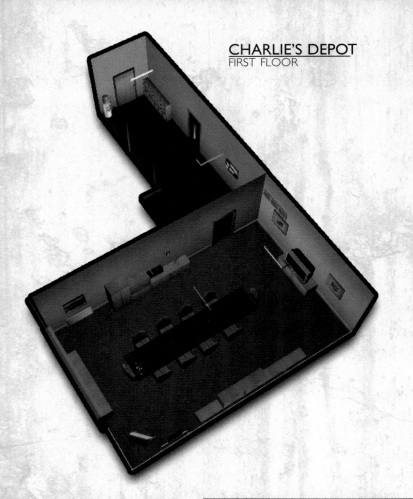

E McCormack walks to the other end of the depot and climbs up the stairs. Go down the ladder you climbed up, and backtrack to the front of the depot. Use the same path you took before and you won't be spotted. Wait for McCormack to enter the door on the first floor, then go up the stairs in pursuit to complete the mission.

Stay against the wall of the depot as you make your way to the ladder in the rear.

A

HOSPITAL
GROUND

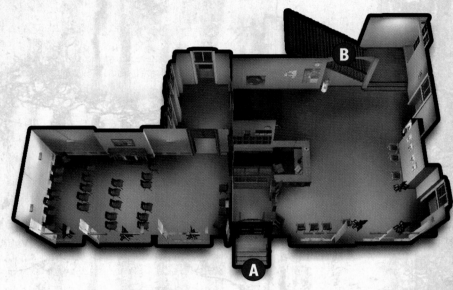

B

A

A You start the mission in front of the depot without a car. Turn left and boost the Range Rover or the Lexus, or run into the street and grab a passing vehicle. You have four minutes of real-time to reach UCL and find Joe's room. Do NOT drive to the entrance you might remember from an earlier mission. Look for a door on the right side of the street, just before the turn to the second entrance.

HOSPITAL
FIRST FLOOR

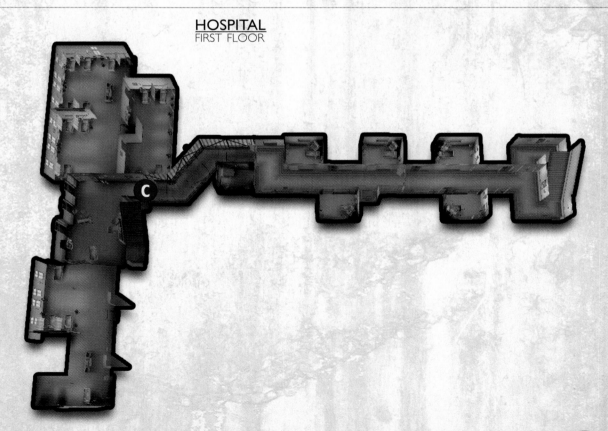

C

B Run into the reception area and immediately climb the stairs to the first floor.

C Turn right at the top and run through the potted-plant hallway. Continue running straight ahead and follow the hallway to the end, where you find the stairs to the second floor.

D Follow the hallway to the room with the guard posted in front, and run into the room to complete the mission.

Waste no time running through the halls of the hospital to find Joe's room on the second floor.

You'll rarely make it to Joe before the timer starts ticking. An indicator of the difficulty of this mission.

HOSPITAL
SECOND FLOOR

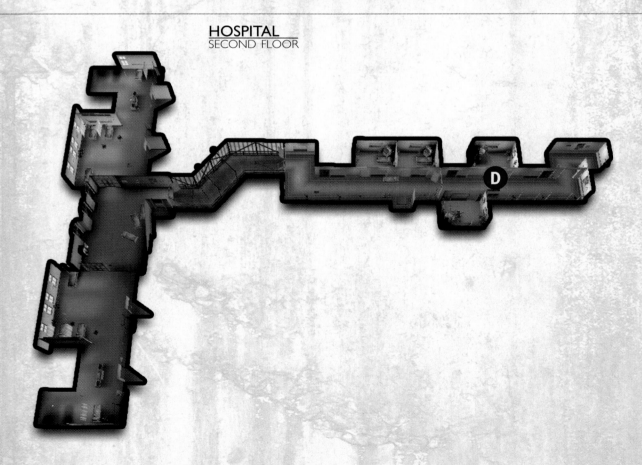

WALKTHROUGH

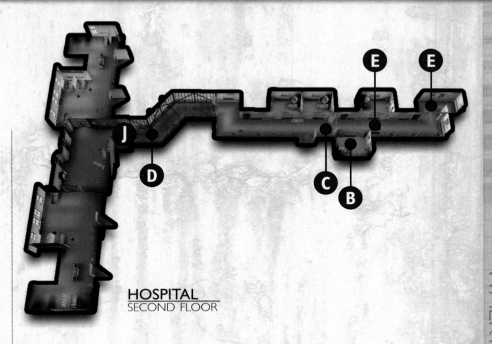

HOSPITAL
SECOND FLOOR

Run outside of Joe's room and intercept the hitman in the brown suit, then take out several more thugs down the hall. One of them runs away, which naturally provokes you into giving chase with a police escort behind you.

A Please do not, under any circumstances, enter the room of a bedridden patient and shoot the patient until he flatlines, or you will doom yourself.

B Two thugs come out of the right-hand doors as you move down the hallway, so welcome their surprise appearances with a hail of gunfire. A third thug appears and attacks from behind as you pass through the glass doors.

C A shotgun-armed thug blasts you as you come around the final corner of the glass walkway (unless you already killed him in the earlier commotion).

D The doors at the end of the walkway are bolted shut, so backtrack to Joe's room and walk past it, down the stairs to the first floor.

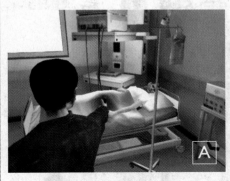

If you engage in the activity depicted here, you are beyond redemption, and we can only pray for you.

Thugs lurk behind many of the doors on the second (and first) floors.

There is some good news to this: at least you're being shot in a hospital.

Joe has a visitor, but this one is most definitely not bringing flowers and a card.

Thugs also attack you from behind at several points during your explorations.

WALKTHROUGH

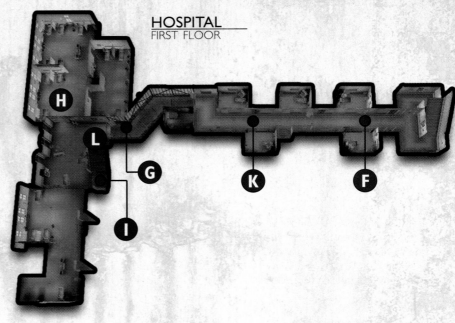

HOSPITAL
FIRST FLOOR

E Two thugs attack from the other end of the hallway. Pick them off from long range with your pistols.

F Run forward, through the glass hall way, and shoot a group of thugs at the opposite end.

G Turn right after exiting the hallway and shoot several thugs inside the room. There's a fat bastard around the corner to the right. Shoot him until he runs away, then blast his cohorts.

H Return to the end of the hallway and go up the stairs, back to the second floor.

I Patrol the hallway, shoot a thug or two, and return down the stairs to the first floor.

J Make a final sweep of the first floor and finish off the last of the bad guys, at which point Carter makes a comment.

K Go down the first floor stairs next to the glass hallway, greet your fellow officers, and head out to the street to begin the next mission.

HOSPITAL
GROUND FLOOR

You can't kill the big-boned thug in this room, but you can get him running as fast as he can manage.

Return to the first floor for a second helping of bad guys. Clean them up to complete the first mission.

Carter's fellow officers promise practice their synchronous gun-holding routine while Carter runs off to shoot more people.

LONDON

I Run out to the street and grab a fast car for the drive to Scoresby Street. You have nine minutes of real-time to reach the lockup, which should be much more than enough. You'll know you've reached the place when you see three cars parked in front.

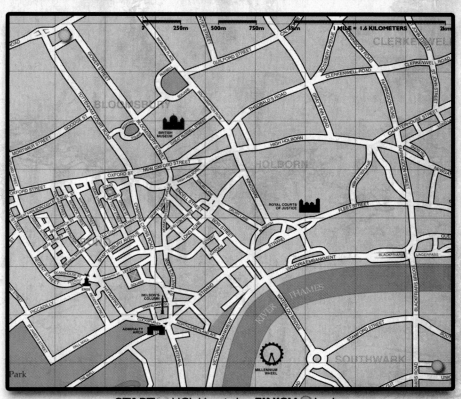

START ○ UCL Hospital   **FINISH** ○ Lockup

With nine minutes to drive from UCL to the lockup, you have absolutely no reason to fail the mission.

Look for a trio of parked cars as irrefutable evidence that you've found the lockup--and that Jolson's boys have beaten you to it.

WALKTHROUGH

WALKTHROUGH

A Approach the lockup and shoot two guards in front. A car screeches down the alley and attempts to ram you from behind. Stay against either wall to avoid being struck, then shoot the two thugs as they get out of the car.

B If you walk near the entrance to the lockup, several thugs run outside to attack you. You can pick them off from a safe distance.

C When the thugs stop coming, run to the entrance and move up against the right side. Press the SQUARE button to shoot around the corner and kill both the thugs (or lean out and shoot them, although blindly firing around the corner is much more fun).

D Run forward into the lockup and three thugs attack: one from underneath the raised car and one on either side of you. Quickly auto-aim and kill each one in turn.

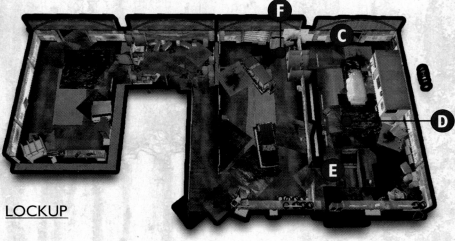

LOCKUP

E Move up against the right side of the doorway (after shooting a thug who attacks from behind you). Fire around the corner with SQUARE to kill the thug. Move around the corner, still pressed against the wall, and lean around the corner to hit two more thugs.

F Two thugs attack from behind as you move into the room. Wheel around and kill them, then run forward and into the corners to find the files and complete the mission.

Use the always enjoyable blind-shot-around-the-corner technique to take out one of the thugs in the lockup.

Two cowardly thugs attack from behind as you enter the final room of the lockup. Turn around and fire away.

LONDON

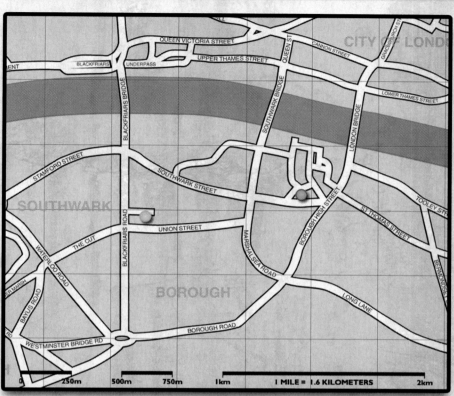

START ◯ Lockup   **FINISH** ◯ Charlie's Warehouse

W alk outside and take the white Lexus to the warehouse, which is a short drive away. Look for a gray wall on the left side of the road with a small gap. Park well away from the gap, then press up against the wall and peek around the corner.

While you've done a lot of driving to and from the warehouse and depot, you've never gone directly from one to another...until now.

Park well away from the gap in the wall (and on the sidewalk, regardless of what you see in this screenshot).

WALKTHROUGH

A Sidestep to the corner of the gap and wait for the two thugs go their separate ways. Run up behind the thug on the right and hog-tie him (X to grab, SQUARE to restrain). Now enter the warehouse and repeat the process with the thug reading the bulletin board.

B Climb the stairs, move through the door, then go down the next set of stairs and hide behind the pallet. Listen in the conversation between the thugs and stay put.

C Wait for all the thugs to disperse, then move up against the door into the next section of the warehouse. Wait as the brown coat-wearing thug chats with his friends and starts walking toward the crates, then move through the door and immediately move up against the crates. Wait for the two thugs to start moving, then grab the green-shirted thug and hog-tie him.

D Run straight ahead and forward until you're almost at the wall, then hide behind the boxes. Wait for two crates to be moved into position near the basement, then run forward and press up against the other side of the new box-stack.

E Wait for one of the thugs to walk down the stairs, then hog-tie the remaining guard from behind and move into the basement.

F Press up against the wall and listen around the corner. Wait for both thugs to walk away.

G Enter the room and hog-tie the green-shirted thug on the right, then run around the corner to complete the mission.

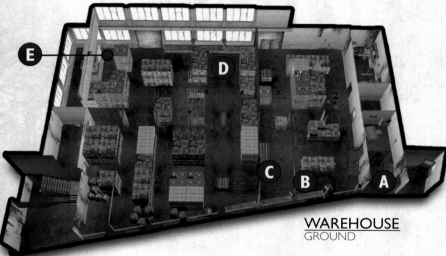

WAREHOUSE
GROUND

When the two thugs break off their witty banter, run up behind the green-clad baddie and tie him up.

WAREHOUSE
BASEMENT

You're almost there. Be patient as the thugs blather, then hog-tie the one on the right and get around the corner.

Start

Immediately draw your weapon and shoot the thug as he charges down the stairs. Proceed up the stairs and shoot two more thugs at the top.

A Hide behind the boxes and pick off the thugs guarding the path to the exit. More thugs will attack from all directions, so head for the exit door.

B A dozen thugs besiege you as you approach the door. Keep shooting them as you make your way outside. A car skids into the warehouse parking lot. Kill the driver as he gets out, and boost the vehicle.

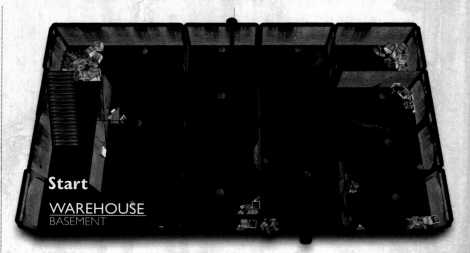

Start

WAREHOUSE
BASEMENT

The warehouse is teeming with thugs as you emerge from the basement. Keep pressing forward and thinning them out.

Shoot the thugs inside the sweet vehicle, then get behind the wheel. Boosting cars just never gets old.

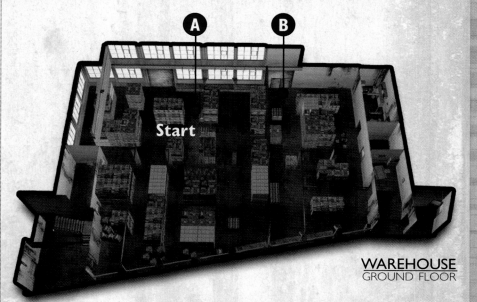

A   **B**

Start

WAREHOUSE
GROUND FLOOR

WALKTHROUGH

LONDON

Bethnal boys will harass you as you leave the warehouse, but most of the drive should be surprisingly straight-forward. Pull into the parking lot of the depot, get out of the car, and run inside.

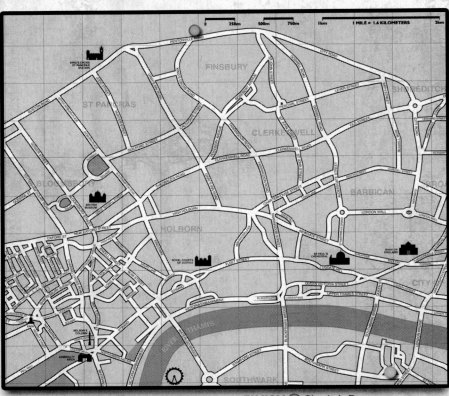

Start

START ○ Charlie's Warehouse   **FINISH** ○ Charlie's Depot

The Bethnal boys run minimal interference during your drive to the depot, which makes them smarter than they look.

A Enter the depot, turn right, and climb the stairs.

B At the top of the stairs, turn right and hog-tie or knock out the thug.

C Turn around and walk out into the depot. Climb down the stairs and hog-tie or knock out the thug.

D Run forward into the depot, staying close to the conveyor belt against the wall so you aren't spotted.

E Turn left and move against the boxes, then sidestep left toward the car until the screen fades out and you complete the mission.

CHARLIE'S DEPOT
GROUND FLOOR

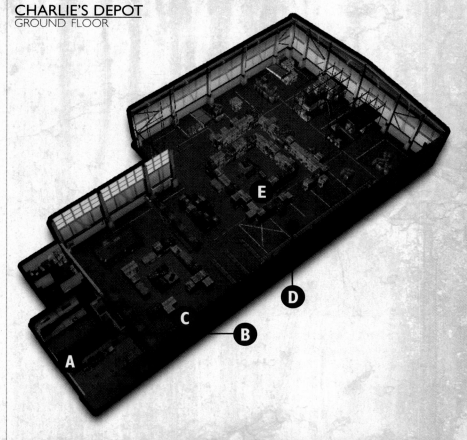

WALKTHROUGH

LONDON

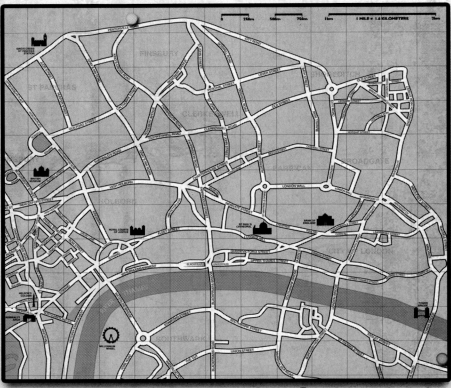

START ◯ Charlie's Depot   **FINISH** ◯ Sol Vita

Lean around the corner and shoot the middle red crate to blow it up and send one thug flying, then finish off the other.

① Leave the warehouse, kill the thug at the end of the parking lot, and boost his Lexus.

② You have 10 and a half minutes of real-time to reach the Sol Vita, which is much more than enough. When you reach the dock entrance, follow the road to the parking lot in front of the Sol Vita.

Start

Shooting explosives is another activity that never gets old, no matter how frequently indulged in.

① One of Jake's cohorts very kindly waits outside the depot with a Lexus. Show your gratitude by giving him a quick death.

② Ten and a half minutes is plenty of time to make the drive, even with gang members trying their best to delay you.

② Go through the dock entrance and drive as close as you can to the Sol Vita, which will never be confused with a cruise ship.

WALKTHROUGH

A Run up the ramp and clobber or hog-tie the thug at the top. Take the AK-47 and lean up against the container.

B Sidestep right to the corner, then watch and wait as a forklift parks a pallet of explosives next to the thugs. Wait until four pallets have been moved into place, then lean around the corner and shoot one of the pallets to trigger them all to explode and kill about a dozen thugs in the process. This saves you from engaging in a protracted (and probably fatal) fire-fight.

C Move toward the bridge of the ship, shooting several thugs who attack from behind the containers.

D Run up the stairs on the left side of the ship and shoot at Jake as he comes around the corner. Jake dashes away, so follow him around.

E Enter the quarters and Jake dashes away again. Blast three thugs as you follow Jake around the corner.

F Climb up the stairs to the mess and engage in a fierce and bloody shootout with a group of thugs at the top. Approach the door to the deck and turn around to kill a shotgun-toting thug who attacks you from behind.

G On the deck, turn and shoot the thug near the ladder then climb up.

Jake dashes away as you enter the ship quarters, leaving behind a couple of flunkies for you to pump full of bullets.

You'll have to wait for a couple of minutes at the start of the mission, but your patience will be rewarded with a massive kill.

The chain-detonation kills most of the thugs. Walk forward and mow down who-ever's left.

The group shootout in the ship mess is as frantic an action sequence as you'll ever experience.

WALKTHROUGH

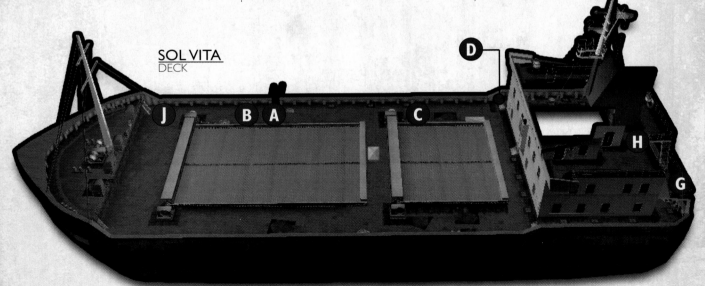

SOL VITA
DECK

H Move up against the blue wall and sidestep right until you see Jake. He swoops away on a crane, leaving two thugs behind to kill you. Kill them both and backtrack through the mess and quarters to the main deck.

I You're attacked by two thugs from around the corner as you reach the bottom of the stairs into the quarters. Shoot 'em both and proceed into the main deck.

J Jake is at the rear of the deck, walking back and forth. Approach him on the side of the deck with the containers to keep yourself hidden from view. Kill a stray thug, then approach the rail and blast Jake with everything you've got. Drop Jake to complete the mission.

As you return to the ship quarters, thugs return to try and kill you again. Suffice to say, they'll fail.

SOL VITA
QUARTERS

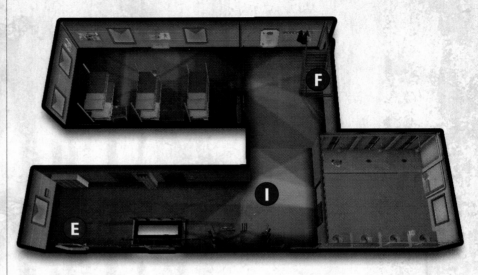

SOL VITA
MESS

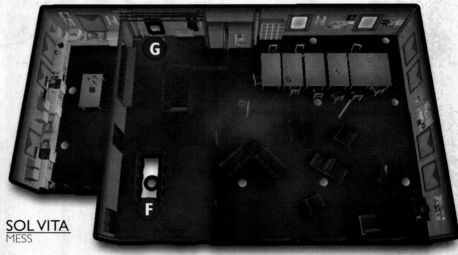

Run behind the containers on the right side of the Sol Vita to prevent Jake from getting a clear shot at you.

Make sure you have plenty of ammo before starting to blast Jake with both barrels (or an AK-47, although the pistols are superior).

You have three minutes of real-time to get out of the Sol Vita. Immediately run down the stairs and forward, blasting a thug as you reach the bottom.

A As you reach the corner, an explosion tears down the steel walkway and blocks the passage. Continue forward.

B Blast the thug and climb the stairs.

C Run along the railing and down the stairs into the hold. Shoot a thug as you come around the corner.

D Proceed through the cargo hold to the door, blasting thugs as you go. Take a rest if you're about to die; otherwise, keep moving forward.

E Blast several passing thugs as you reach the door. You can also shoot the barrels outside to kill them in the blast.

F Turn left as you re-enter the corridor and run forward, shooting the idiotic thugs.

G Sidestep up to the corner of the engine room passage, then lean out and kill the thugs guarding it.

H Enter the engine room and kill the warring gangsters inside. Climb up the stairways and walk out to the deck to complete the mission.

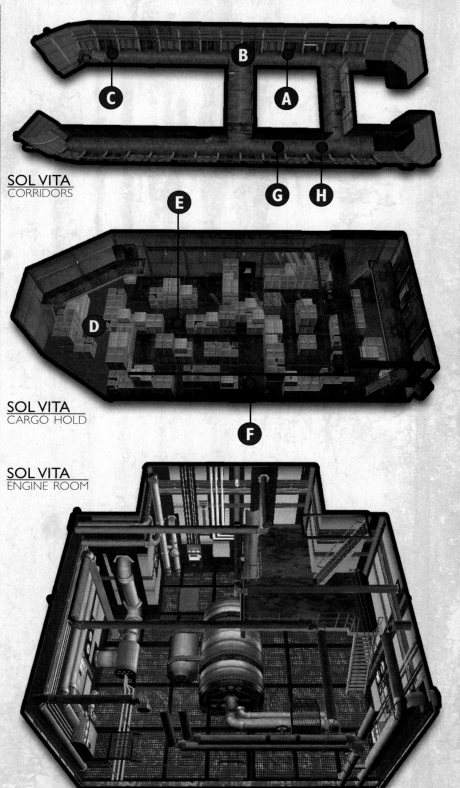

SOL VITA
CORRIDORS

SOL VITA
CARGO HOLD

SOL VITA
ENGINE ROOM

04 | THE WEAPONS LIST
PART IV

WEAPONS LIST

A

C

E

There are eight weapons in The Getaway, four each in two categories: guns and clubs. (Missile weapons and melee weapons, to use the technical terminology.) While the guns have varying firing rates, range, and accuracy, the clubs are identical in function, if not in appearance.

The Getaway doesn't display how much ammunition you have, but as long as you keep picking up fresh weapons to replace your spent ones, you won't have to worry about it.

A To take a gun, simply walk over it. If you have one pistol and walk over a pistol, you take the second handgun; if you already have two, you leave it on the ground.

B If you're carrying a high-powered weapon (shotgun, AK-47, or MP5), you won't take another gun--and if you're carrying a gun, you won't take a club. Drop your high-powered gun or put away your pistol(s) to take the club.

C High-powered guns, unlike pistols, can't be stashed in your jacket, and thus draw immediate police attention. High-powered guns also can't be reloaded; once you're out, you automatically throw the spent weapon to the ground and draw your trusty pistol(s).

D Press and hold R1 to automatically target an attacker. If there are multiple attackers, press R1 to toggle between them.

E Press and hold R2 to manually aim a gun. You turn very slowly when manually aiming; if you want to aim at someone or something behind you, turn around and then aim, instead of aiming and then slowly turning around. If you're injured, your aim wavers as you sway back and forth.

F You can shoot a car engine until the car bursts into flame, you can shoot

and flatten tires, and you can shoot a surprising number of objects. Aim and fire at bottles, balloons, barrels (especially the red ones filled with explosives), et cetera. You'll be amazed at how much damage you can wreak.

G To use a club, simply walk up to an attacker and press SQUARE. If you're injured, your swing takes longer to connect. You can also press SQUARE while holding a gun to pistol-whip or gun-butt your enemy. Most clubs kill an opponent with a single swat, while pistol-whipping or gun-butting requires a couple of swings.

A

B

D

F

G

This is the standard weapon in *The Getaway*; Mark Hammond and DC Carter are always armed with at least one pistol, and can pick up a second. It's the best weapon in the game, with a solid rate of fire (excellent if you have two), great range, and uncanny accuracy. You can go through the entire game using just your pistols and have no trouble; all other weapons are essentially optional.

Pistol

This is a high-powered weapon with poor range, a horrible rate of fire, and almost instant kills; it only takes one or two shots to slay an attacker, depending on which portion of his body is struck by the initial blast. Shotgun blasts can even maim or kill multiple attackers at once, if they're close together. Shotguns are very entertaining, but not very practical; take another weapon if one is available. Look for shotguns in the cold, dead hands of deceased thugs.

Shotgun

This high-powered weapon has good range, poor accuracy, and a blazing rate of fire. It's superior to the shotgun in close-range situations, since there are no reloading pauses, but it's definitely not a weapon of choice for long-range sniping. AK-47s are used by various gang members.

AK-47

The best weapon in the game, the MP5 gets top marks in every category. You can even pick up and use two of them at once, allowing you to cut down enemies in the blink of an eye. MP5s are obtained from the bodies of special police forces in a few (too few) of the missions.

MP5

Used by Triads and Yardies.

Baseball Bat

Found in only a few missions.

Cleaver

Another rare melee weapon.

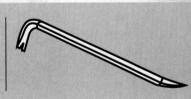

Crowbar

Look for a rozzer with a funny hat patrolling the sidewalk. Any rozzer will do. Draw your gun to provoke the rozzer into drawing his baton, then kill him and take his weapon. Thank you very much!

Police Baton

WEAPONS LIST

05 | THE VEHICLE CHART
PART V

VEHICLE CHART

There are dozens of vehicles in *The Getaway*, and you can drive all of them. When you see a car you want to drive, simply approach the vehicle and press CIRCLE to get inside--usually at gunpoint. Each vehicle has its own acceleration, top speed, and handling characteristics, but the rule of thumb is this: the fancier and more expensive the car, the faster it goes and the better it handles. What follows is an illustrated list of two dozen of *The Getaway*'s most common vehicles, which you'll see in every section of London; for the locations of ten secret/unique vehicles, check out the Tour of London section.

#	✓	CAR NAME / MODEL
01	☐	Black Cab
02	☐	Brabus
03	☐	Daihatsu Sirion
04	☐	Dennis Fire Engine
05	☐	Double Decker Bus
06	☐	Fiat Punto
07	☐	Honda Civic
08	☐	Jensen SV8
09	☐	Lexus IS200
10	☐	Lexus LS
11	☐	Lorry
12	☐	Lotus Elite

#	✓	CAR NAME / MODEL
13	☐	MG ZT
14	☐	Nissan Micra
15	☐	Nissan Skyline
16	☐	Police Vectra
17	☐	Range Rover
18	☐	Renault Laguna
19	☐	Rover SD1
20	☐	Saab 900
21	☐	Saab 93
22	☐	Toyota Hiace
23	☐	TVR Cerbera
24	☐	Unmarked Police Vectra

3 Daihatsu Sirion

1 Black Cab

4 Dennis Fire Engine

2 Brabus

5 Double Decker Bus	10 Lexus LS	15 Nissan Skyline	20 Saab 900
6 Fiat Punto	11 Lorry	16 Police Vectra	21 Saab 93
7 Honda Civic	12 Lotus Elite	17 Range Rover	22 Toyota Hiace
8 Jensen SV8	13 MG ZT	18 Renault Laguna	23 TVR Cerbera
9 Lexus IS200	14 Nissan Micra	19 Rover SDI	24 Unmarked Police Vectra

06 | THE TOUR OF LONDON
PART VI

TOUR OF LONDON

Defeat all 24 missions of *The Getaway*, and you unlock Free Roaming mode, which is accessed from the Extra Features menu. Put simply, Free Roaming allows you to drive around London at your leisure, without any missions or time limits. Certain rules of the game still apply: police chase you if you break the law (which includes reckless driving), and gangsters are angered if you attempt to boost their cars.

What follows is a list of some of London's major landmarks, followed by directions on how to find *The Getaway*'s ten top-secret cars--many of which can only be found in Free Roaming.

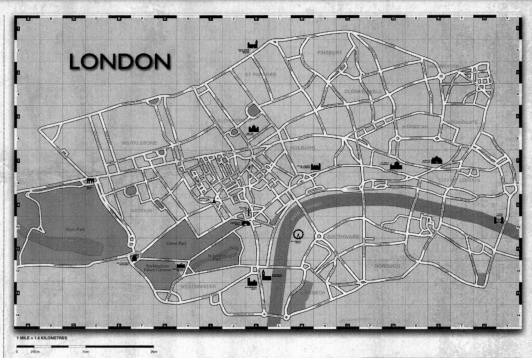

LONDON

1 MILE = 1.6 KILOMETRES

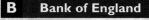

A   Admiralty Arch

Designed by Aston Webb (who also designed the front of Buckingham Palace) and constructed between 1906 and 1910, it was originally designed as a memorial to Queen Victoria.

B   Bank of England

The central bank of the United Kingdom was founded in 1694, nationalized in 1946, and gained operational independence in 1997.

C   British Museum

Designed by Robert Smirke, the British Museum took an incredible 24 years to build (1823 to 1847). The Museum houses the King's Library and many of the world's finest works of art. Among the exhibits are the Rosetta Stone, the Egyptian Hall, and the Sutton Hoo treasure.

D   Buckingham Palace

This has served as the official London residence of Britain's sovereigns since 1837. It evolved from a town house that was built for the Duke of Buckingham in 1703. Today, it is the Queen's official residence. Buckingham Palace was designed with the Marble Arch as its main entrance, but the Arch was later moved to Hyde Park. Buckingham Palace has over 600 rooms, some of which were opened to the public in 1993. Directly across from the Palace is the Victoria Memorial, designed by Thomas Brock and built in 1911.

E   Houses of Parliament

Also known as the Palace of Westminster, the original structure was built in the 11th century under the direction of Edward the Confessor, then rebuilt after a fire in 1834. The House of Commons is a group of elected officials, while the House of Lords are hereditary and nominated for leadership. The Houses of Parliament are most famous for Big Ben, a 13.8-ton bell inside the Palace's 316-foot clock tower (NOT the clock tower itself). Big Ben was likely named after the bulky Welshman Sir Benjamin Hall, whose name was inscribed on the bell upon its creation.

the Getaway

F Hyde Park Corner

The triple-gate entry to Hyde Park was designed by Decimus Burton. There are several sculptures across the street from the entry.

G King's Cross Station

Designed by Lewis Cubitt and built in 1851 and 1852, the Kings Cross Station was erected on the former site of a former hospital. The clock tower is 120 feet high, with clock dials measuring 9' in diameter. The Station originally included a six-story granary able to hold 60,000 sacks of corn.

H London Eye

The world's largest Ferris wheel, built in celebration of the new millennium, the London Eye carries 800 passengers at a time in 32 glass capsules to a height of 450 feet. On a clear day, passengers can see 25 miles in every direction from the Eye's highest point.

I Marble Arch

Designed by John Nash, who was largely inspired by the Constantine Arch in Rome, the Arch was built in 1828 as the chief entrance to Buckingham Palace. When the Palace was extended in 1851, the Arch was moved to its current site as an entrance to Hyde Park. Various road changed have left the Arch on a traffic island. A bronze equestrian statue of King George IV was meant to have been displayed atop the Arch, but the sculpture was relocated to Trafalgar Square.

J Royal Courts of Justice

Completed in 1881, the Royal Courts (which house the Supreme Court of Justice for England and Wales) have been called "the last great Gothic public building in London."

J St. Paul's Cathedral

The current Cathedral, which has the second-largest dome in the world (after St. Peter's Basilica in Rome), is the fifth church on the site. After the Great Fire of London in 1666, the Cathedral was redesigned by Christopher Wren and completed in 1711.

K Statue of Eros

Located in Piccadilly Circus, the Statue of Eros was originally called the Shaftesbury Monument, having been erected as a momument to the philanthropist Lord Shaftesbury. The fountain is made of bronze, but Eros is made of aluminum, a rare and novel material when the Statue was built in the late 19th century. In 1994, the Statue was vandalized by a drunken tourist who climbed on the figure and bent it, requiring a lengthy repair.

L Tower Bridge

Built over eight years by the combined effort of 432 construction workers, the Tower Bridge is 11,000 tons of steel, covered with Cornish granite and Portland stone. Tower Bridge was the largest bascule (French for "see-saw") bridge of its era, able to lift each of its bascules to an 86-degree angle using massive steam engines. In 1952, a London bus jumped from one bascule to another when the Bridge began to rise with the bus still on it.

M Trafalgar Square

The centerpiece of the Square of London is Nelson's Column, built from 1840 to 1843, and standing 185 feet high. The four lions at the base of the Column represent the four great naval victories achieved by British naval hero Admiral Horatio Nelson, who lost an arm, an eye, and ultimately his life in military service. Nelson's final and most famous battle was fought off the Spanish cape of Trafalgar, when he defeated Napoleon and the French and Spanish fleet.

N Westminster Abby

The most visited religious site in England, Westminster Abbey is the final resting place of kings, statesmen, scientists and warriors; among its permanent residents are Charles Darwin, Charles Dickens, and Geoffrey Chaucer. Westminster Abbey has seen the coronation of virtually every English monarch since William the Conqueror, and was also the site for the 1997 funeral of the Princess of Wales.

1   306 Street Racer

This car can be found in the normal and Free Roaming modes. Start on the Westminster Bridge, driving west (toward Big Ben). Drive past Big Ben and turn left at the intersection. Drive forward until you reach the round-about, then turn right. You should see a long stretch of blue boards on the right side of the road, followed by a small gap with a pile of card-board boxes in it. Drive into the gap and into an under-ground car park with the 306 in the corner, behind the hut.

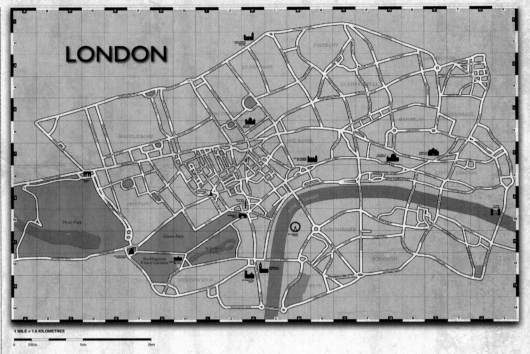

LONDON

1 MILE = 1.6 KILOMETRES

2   Golf Cart

This vehicle can only be found in the Free Roaming mode. Make your way to the front gate of the Mansion (see below), then turn right and drive forward. Watch the left side of the road for two gray posts; drive through the posts and into Hyde Park. Drive for-ward on the path until it splits into two, with a large clearing in front of you. Drive into the clearing and look for two large hedges on the right; the Cart is parked behind them.

3   Hi-Jet Pick-Up

This car can be found in the normal and Free Roaming modes. Make your way to the front gate of the Mansion (see below), then turn around and drive straight ahead, down the road. You'll eventually see a trail leading into Hyde Park. Turn onto the trail and drive straight ahead until you see a blue hut. Look behind the hut to find the Hi-Jet Pick-Up.

4   Lotus Esprit

This car can be found in the normal and Free Roaming modes. From Charlie's Depot, drive through the gates and turn right. Drive straight ahead a LONG way, until you spot a turnout on the right side of the road. Follow the turnout to the end, then drive behind the building. Look for an alcove on the right; the Esprit is parked inside.

5   Mansion

There are four secret cars at the Mansion, which can only be found in the Free Roaming mode: Go-Kart, Lotus M250, Skyline, and TVR. From the start of Free Roaming, pull a 180. Drive forward and turn right at the T intersection. Drive forward and turn right at the four-way intersection. Drive forward until you reach the Marble Arch; follow the traffic left, then immediately follow the road around to the right. Drive forward and continue going straight ahead at the junction, keeping Hyde Park on your left. Keep going to the end of the road, where you reach a grass-covered road island. Drive straight over the island and through the opened gate (which is closed in the regular gameplay mode). Follow the path to the Mansion, where the Skyline and TVR are parked in front, and the Go-Kart and Lotus M250 are parked in the garage.

6   MZ2

You start with this car in Free Roaming mode.

7   Saab 9X

Drive to the lowest level of the NCP Carpark in Chinatown.

8   Skyline (White)

This car can be found in the normal and Free Roaming modes. From the entrance to Charlie's Warehouse, turn right, right again, and left onto the main road. Drive forward and take the first right turn (with a light-blue shop called "Minty" on the corner). Drive ahead to an intersection and turn right, driving against the flow of traffic. Watch the left side of the road for a pile of cardboard boxes; walk behind the boxes to find the Skyline.

9   Tank

This vehicle can be found in the normal and Free Roaming modes. From the front gate of Buckingham Palace, facing the Victoria Memorial, turn right and drive through the posts and over the small area of glass. Turn left at the junction and drive forward. Watch the right side of the road for a group of brown autumnal leaves. Go through the gate near these trees to find the Tank. In the Free Roaming mode only, press L3 to fire the Tank's cannon.

the Getaway

WHERE COPS DON'T DEAL

CRIMINALS DON'T BARGAIN

AND CRIME BOSSES DON'T NEGOTIATE